ISBN 978-0-265-99796-3
PIBN 10920950

THE LABOR LEGISLATION
OF UTAH

WITH SPECIAL REFERENCE TO THE PERIOD
OF STATEHOOD

BY

OWEN FRANKLIN BEAL, A. M.

SUBMITTED IN PARTIAL FULFILLMENT OF THE REQUIREMENTS
FOR THE DEGREE OF DOCTOR OF PHILOSOPHY
IN THE
FACULTY OF POLITICAL SCIENCE
COLUMBIA UNIVERSITY

THE LABOR LEGISLATION
OF UTAH

WITH SPECIAL REFERENCE TO THE PERIOD
OF STATEHOOD

BY

OWEN FRANKLIN BEAL, A. M.

SUBMITTED IN PARTIAL FULFILLMENT OF THE REQUIREMENTS
FOR THE DEGREE OF DOCTOR OF PHILOSOPHY
IN THE
FACULTY OF POLITICAL SCIENCE
COLUMBIA UNIVERSITY

LOGAN, UTAH
1922

FOREWORD

The purpose of this study is to show what has been done in the field of labor legislation in Utah, having special reference to the period of statehood.

An effort has been made to present in orderly arrangement the scope and general content of the labor laws without giving the details and legal verbiage of these enactments.

It has also been thought advisable to give the industrial beginnings and development in Utah, as a helpful background to this study. This brief preliminary survey, however, of the industrial life of Utah, merely indicates the channels into which the energies and resources of the state have been directed with the purpose in view of pointing out more clearly the trend that labor legislation has taken in this commonwealth.

It may also be well to state that no record has been found of any special investigation or research in this particular field which covers specifically the State of Utah, therefore, the writer has had to rely largely upon his own investigations.

It is to be hoped, however, that this study may prove helpful in connection with the further improvement and administration of the labor laws of this state. In any event, this subject is in itself of interest since it forms a part of the larger history of labor legislation in the United States. The relation of many matters here discussed to the larger problems of Industrial Relations, in which so many students are now interested, will be apparent.

CONTENTS

PART I

INTRODUCTION

CHAPTER I

PART II

TERRITORIAL PERIOD

1850-1896

CHAPTER II

PART III

PERIOD OF STATEHOOD

1896-1921

CHAPTER III

6　　　　　　　　　　　　　　*Contents*

PART I
INTRODUCTION

THE LABOR LEGISLATION
OF UTAH

CHAPTER I

THE INDUSTRIAL BEGINNINGS AND DEVELOPMENT
IN UTAH

1. HISTORICAL BEGINNINGS OF UTAH

(1) THE WESTWARD MOVEMENT

In the opening page of his book, entitled, "The Last American Frontier", Professor Paxson interestingly refers to the story of the United States as representing a series of frontiers, which to quote his words, "the hand of man has reclaimed from nature and the savage, and which courage and foresight have gradually transformed from desert waste to virile commonwealth."[1]

He further points out in this same opening chapter that, "the winning of the first frontier established in America its first white settlements". Later, he tells us, was—"added the frontier of the Alleghanies and the Ohio, of the Mississippi and the Missouri," and then finally, "the winning of the last frontier completed the conquest of the continent."[2]

The colonization of Utah had its beginning in connection with the winning of the last American frontier; the frontier which extended the boundaries of the United States to the Pacific coast.

Of this last great western migration, the historian referred to above, records in his work that the first impulse beckoning colonists from the Mississippi and Missouri across the western plains was, "chiefly conquest, with Oregon as the result". "Religion", he tells us, "was the next, producing Utah", and then he informs us, "the lust for gold followed close upon the second, calling into life California, and then in a later decade sprinkling little camps over all the mountain West."[3]

[1] Paxson, F. L., The Last American Frontier, p. 1.
[2] Ibid., p. 1.
[3] Ibid., p. 103.

(2) THE UTAH PIONEERS

Prior to 1847 a small number of Americans had settled among Indians and Spaniards upon the Pacific coast, but no permanent settlement had been made in Utah. In the spring of this year, however, a company of Mormon pioneers from the State of Illinois set out for the Far West. In July of the same year, 1847, they entered the valley of the Great Salt Lake and "planted the first of the inland settlements in the heart of the desert".[1]

This remote valley of the Great Salt Lake, though far from the borders of civilization, and which originally had little to invite and much to repel;[2] a seemingly inhospitable region, became an oasis in the American desert.[3]

A new civilization grew rapidly in this inter-mountain region. The first party of pioneers was followed by other companies and within a year nearly four thousand people had settled in Utah. By 1850, nearly twelve thousand people had crossed the plains and settled here. Salt Lake City became the forerunner—center or parent city, so to speak, of many thriving communities in the valleys of the Rocky Mountains.

The trials, hardships, and difficulties of the early pioneers to redeem the desert and bring progress to these parts offer a field of study of much interest in itself, the details of which extend beyond the purpose of this study. In passing, however, let it be said that their spirit of cooperation, and unity of purpose to obtain economic results; their industry and frugality, have drawn praise from the pen of more than one impartial observer.[4]

---

[1]Paxson, F. L., The Last American Frontier, p. 103.

[2]Immigrants passing through Utah spoke of it as a mean land, "hard, dry and fit only for the plodding, thrifty, sober Mormons." (See Bancroft, H. H., History of Utah, p. 723.)

[3]Yet this land which seemed barren beyond redemption, and which seemingly offered so few prospects of being reclaimed, yielded on less than 17 acres of its soil, in 1880, some 1,250 bushels of grain. (See Bancroft, H. H., History of Utah, p. 724.)

[4]Edward W. Tullidge in his book, "Utah and Her Founders", (Chapter 13, pp. 216-233), gives a number of sketches of the early days of Utah as viewed by United States government officials and English travelers. One account is quoted from Captain Stansbury who was sent out by the government to survey the lakes; in company with Lieutenant Gunnison.

In his official report he says, in part: 'The founding, within the space of three years, of a large and flourishing community, upon a spot so remote from the abodes of men, so completely shut out by natural barriers from the rest of the world, so entirely unconnected by water-courses with either of the oceans that wash the shores of this continent, a country

Professor Paxon has the following to say concerning the pioneers of Utah:

"Its people were of the stuff that had colonized the Middle West and won a foothold in Oregon, but nowhere did an emigration so nearly create a land which it enjoyed as here."[1] Again, he says in his chapter on the Mormon pioneers that their leadership was not excelled by any people passing over the Oregon trail to the Far West.[2]

A more graphic picture of this early period in Utah has been given by a well known historian of this western country, Hubert Howe Bancroft. In referring to the colonizing genius of the Mormon people, which he tells us was manifested from the beginning of their settlement in the inter-mountain region of the Far West, he has this to say, in part:

"In all the stages of her existence, Utah has been constantly expanding, her growth, far from depleting her resources, only added to her strength. Originally one of the most barren spots on the face of nature, with nothing to attract even attention, the land has become as fruitful a field, and her people as busy a commonwealth, as can be found, with few exceptions elsewhere on the Pacific slope."[3]

After describing somewhat the topography of this section— the unkindly soil, the slight rainfall and the like, he again writes, "amid this forbidding and inhospitable region the Mormons built

offering no advantages of inland navigation or of foreign commerce, but, on the contrary, isolated by vast uninhabited deserts, and only to be reached by long, painful, and often hazardous journeys by land, presents an anomaly so very peculiar, that it deserves more than a passing notice. In this young and prosperous country of ours, where cities grow up in a day, and states spring up in a year, the successful planting of a colony, where the natural advantages have been such as to hold out the promise of adequate reward to the projectors, would have excited no surprise; but the success of an enterprise under circumstances so at variance with all our preconceived ideas of its probability, may well be considered one of the most remarkable incidents of the present age.

'Their admirable system of combining labor, while each has his own property, in lands and tenements, and the proceeds of his industry, the skill in dividing off the lands, and conducting the irrigating canals to supply the wants of rain, which rarely falls between April and October; the cheerful manner in which every one applies himself industriously, but not laboriously; the complete reign of good neighborhood and quiet in house and fields, form themes for admiration to the stranger coming from the dark, and sterile recesses of the mountain gorges into this flourishing valley, and he is struck with wonder at the immense results, produced in so short a time, by a handful of individuals.'

[1]Paxon, F. L., The Last American Frontier, pp. 99-100.
[2]Ibid., p. 99.
[3]Bancroft, H. H., History of Utah, p. 691.

up their settlements, which, nevertheless, grew with a steady and stalwart growth. As year followed year, the magic wand of progress touched into life these barren and sandgirt solitudes, and in their place sprang up a country with the wealth of gardens and granaries, of mines and mills, of farms and factories".[1][*]

2. GEOGRAPHIC FEATURES

The topography of Utah can possibly best be described as a land of mountains, valleys, and plateaus. The eastern portion of the state consists of broad, elevated plateaus cut by canyons and narrow streams and valleys. The remaining western portion is lower and lies within the Great Basin, and is characterized by broad nearly level areas which in turn are interrupted by mountain ranges running north and south throughout the state.[2]

The Wasatch Range extends north and south throughout the central part of Utah, and at the western base of this range is located Salt Lake City, Ogden, Provo, and a number of smaller towns. The Uinta Range runs east and west through the northern part, and small detached mountain ranges are found throughout the state. The land suitable for cultivation lies in the valleys between these ranges.

Only a small part of Utah lies at an altitude of less than 4000 feet above sea-level, and the plateau summits rise to an elevation of from nine, ten, to even eleven thousand feet.

The cities and towns are built on the banks of the streams in the valleys, and the high plateau regions are used largely for grazing purposes, as well as for the wealth they offer in the way of timber lands and mineral deposits.

---

[1]Bancroft, H. H., History of Utah, p. 692.
[*]NOTE:—It may be well to state that Bancroft gained his impressions concerning Utah and her people by personal observations on the ground.

In a somewhat extensive work, including some 700 pages, he gives the history of Utah up to the latter part of the eighties, that is, for the greater part of the territorial period.

In the preface to his history he mentions the fact that the majority of those writing about Utah attempt to make out a case rather than to state the facts. Most of these works, to quote his words, "are written in a sensational style and for the purpose of deriving profit by pandering to a vitiated public taste and are wholly unreliable as to fact." (Bancroft, H. H., History of Utah. Preface, v-xi.)

[2]See Whitney, Orson, F., Popular History of Utah, C. I.

(1) CLIMATE

On account of the diversity in the topography of Utah, it has a somewhat wide range of climatic conditions. Extreme cold weather may occur on the high plateaus, during the winter months, while in the valleys a much milder climate prevails.

The normal annual temperature for Utah is about 47.8 degrees. The normal temperature for January, the midwinter month, is about 25.7 degrees, while the normal temperature for the midsummer month of July is recorded as 71.1 degrees. The normal annual precipitation is about 12.75 inches.[1]

(2) SOIL

The alluvium of the basin region, washed from the high plateaus and mountain ranges furnishes rich soil which produces good crops where irrigated.[2]

(3) LAKES AND RIVERS

The largest body of water in the state is Great Salt Lake which is some eighty miles long and about forty miles in breadth. There are also a number of fresh water lakes—Utah Lake being the largest—and a number of small rivers.

3. GOVERNMENT

(1) ORGANIZATION OF UTAH TERRITORY

Utah is part of the territory which the government of the United States acquired from Mexico by the Treaty of Guadalupe Hidalgo, in 1848.

The people of Utah early expressed a desire to see their new territory brought into the union of states. In the year 1849, a convention was held in Salt Lake City, for the purpose of drawing up a constitution for a state government.

A constitution was drawn up by the members of this convention and along with a memorial was sent to Washington. The memorial asked Congress to admit their new territory as the

---

[1]Report of the State Industrial Commission of Utah, 1917-1918, p. 229. (Article on climate by Cecil Alter, Meteorologist, U. S. Weather Bureau.)

[2]In 1917 Utah produced an average of 13.5 tons of sugar beets per acre. The average for the United States as a whole was 10.6 tons per acre. Statistics and Resources of Utah, 1917, p. 19.

State of Deseret.[1]   The United States Congress, however, did not grant the people statehood, but organized, in 1850, the Territory of Utah,[2] and appointed Brigham Young governor.[3]

The limits of the territory were extensive.   The southern boundary was placed at the "37th parallel of north latitude," and on the west, the territory was bounded—"by the State of California, on the north by the Territory of Oregon; and on the east by the summits of the Rocky Mountains."[4]

Later, as Congress had provided, there was a contraction of the original boundaries by the creation of several new territories. Nevada was formed out of the western end of Utah, and further partitions of the area of the territory occurred when Congress established the territories of Colorado, Idaho, and Wyoming.[5]

(2) UTAH AS A STATE

Utah was received as a state into the Union in 1896, entering as the forty-fifth state.

The state occupies a rectangular area of about 84,990 square miles, of which 2,806 are water surface.   The northeast corner of the rectangle is cut off by the state of Wyoming, and Colorado forms the remaining eastern boundary, while Nevada borders the state on the west, with Idaho and Arizona lying to the north and south.   It ranks tenth in size among the states, with a maximum length of about 345 miles north and south and a maximum width of about 280 miles east and west.[6]

4. THE PEOPLE

(1) GROWTH OF POPULATION

The story of the people of Utah is in large part the history of the Mormons who entered this inter-mountain region in 1847. The pioneers, however, merely started sparse settlements in the valleys of Utah.   Their numbers were increased from year to

[1]Before being admitted as a territory, Utah was called "Deseret", a word used to signify industry.

[2]The word "Utah" comes from "Eutaw", the name of an Indian tribe living in this district.

[3]Young, L. E., Story of Utah, pp. 15-16.

[4]Utah Legislative Assembly, Acts, Resolutions, and Memorials, 1850, pp. 111-119.

[5]See Colorado University Studies, 1916-18, Vol. 4, p. 64, and, Bancroft, H. H., History of Utah, p. 623.

[6]See Encyclopedia Britannica, Vol. 27, pp. 812-819, for a more complete description of Utah.

year largely by emigrants from northwestern Europe, principally
English and Scandinavian emigrants, the dominant parent races
from which the pioneers had themselves descended.[1]

In passing let it also be noted that, while most of the inhabitants of the state are Mormons,[2] there now reside in Utah a
considerable number of people who are not members of the
Mormon Church. In all probability this group of outsiders predominate at Salt Lake City, Ogden, and most of the mining camps.

The people, however, Mormons and Non-Mormons, are united
in building up a prosperous agricultural, and industrial commonwealth.[3*]

The following table shows the growth of population of Utah
by decades from 1850 to 1920.[4**]

Census Year	Population	Increase	Per Cent Increase
1920	449,396	76,045	20.4
1910	373,351	96,602	34.9
1900	276,749	65,970	31.3
1890	210,779	66,816	46.4
1880	143,963	57,177	65.9
1870	86,786	46,513	115.9
1860	40,273	28,893	253.9
1850	11,380		

[1]Bancroft gives in his work on Utah the following interesting description of the people in Salt Lake City in the early territorial period:
"To the student of humanity there were few richer fields for study than
could be found at this period in the Mormon capital, where almost every
state in the Union and every nation in Europe had its representatives.
There were to be seen side by side the tall, sinewy Norwegian, fresh
from his pine forests, the phlegmatic Dane, the stolid, practical German,
the dapper, quickminded Frenchman, the clumsy, dogmatic Englishman,
and the shrewd, versatile American." See Bancroft, H. H., History of
Utah, p. 586.

[2]About seventy-five per cent of the people of the state are Mormons.

[3]Professor Levi Edgar Young writes: "The people of the State
united in building up their commonwealth, and are happy and prosperous. The work of redeeming the desert has been hard; many trials and
difficulties have been met and over-come, and today the result of the
people's work is seen on every hand." (Instructor Literature Series,
Stories of the States, Utah, p. 36.)

*At an earlier period there was religious prejudice over the question
of polygamy. This practice, however, ceased with the issuing of the
"Manifesto" in 1890, and there has followed an era of better feeling
between the Mormons and the Non-Mormons. They have, now, seemingly
"buried the hatchet" and unite as never before politically, economically,
and socially.

[4]Fourteenth Census of the United States, 1920, Population: Utah,
(Advanced Bulletin) p. 1.

**A number of citizens in the state expressed a little disappointment
when they learned that the 1920 population was announced by the
census bureau as 449,446. They had anticipated that the population of

Cities.—According to the Federal Census returns for 1920, Utah has 58 cities. Salt Lake City, the capital and largest city of the state, showed a population of 118,110, and Ogden, the second largest city of the state, had a population of 32,804. Of the total population in 1920, 48 per cent was urban.[1]

Population by Races.—In 1920, the population of Utah was 449,396. Of this number 441,901 were white; 2,936 were Japanese; 2,711 were Indians; 1,446 were Negroes; 342 were Chinese. all others, 60.[2]

Color and Nativity.—In 1920, 245,781 were native whites of native parentage; 139,665 were native whites of foreign or mixed parentage; 56,455 were foreign-born whites; all others 7,495.[3]

Foreign Nationalities.—Of the foreign population of the state in 1920, persons born in England numbered 14,836; in Denmark, 6,970; in Sweden, 6,073; in Germany, 3,589; in Italy, 3,225; in Greece, 3,029; in Scotland, 2,310; in Norway, 2,109; in Netherlands, 1,980; in Switzerland, 1,566; in Wales, 1,304; in Ireland, 1,207; in Austria, 987; in Jugo-Slavia, 836; in Russia, 684; and all other countries, 5,750.[4]

Age.—Of the total population in 1920, 61,375 were under 5 years of age; 56,491, from 5 to 9 years; 51,626, from 10 to 14 years; 43,373, from 15 to 19 years; 161,093, from 20 to 44 years; 74,977, 45 years and over; and 461, age unknown.[5]

5. RESOURCES AND INDUSTRIES

(1) AGRICULTURE

Agriculture is the principal industry in Utah. The founders of the state began a system of irrigation, by leading the water,

---

Utah had reached the half million mark. Yet, as the figures show, there has been a substantial increase in the population of Utah during the last decade. Its rate of growth, 20.4 per cent, represents an increase for the last ten years of 76,045. The state now has more than forty times the population it had when organized as a territory in 1850. In 1850, Utah appeared in the Federal Census for the first time, and its population at that time was 11,380. (See Deseret News, December 20, 1920.)

[1]Fourteenth Census of the United States, 1920, Population, Utah, Advanced Bulletin, entitled, "Number of Inhabitants by Counties and Minor Civil Divisions," p. 2.

[2]Fourteenth Census of the United States, 1920, Population, Utah, Advanced Bulletin, entitled, "Composition and Characteristics of the Population," p. 2.

[3]Ibid., p. 2.

[4]Ibid., p. 5.

[5]Ibid., p. 3.

coming from mountain snows, out on the dry parched soil. By this means the land was made arable and productive, and since that time there has been a rapid and continuous development of this dominant industry.

It is very generally conceded that the founders of Utah were the pioneers of Anglo-Saxon irrigation in arid American.[1] It is hardly an exaggeration to say that probably there are few parts of the world where irrigation has been pushed forward more energetically and systematically and with better results than in Utah. From year to year hundreds of acres are brought under cultivation by means of irrigation projects.[2*]

Where agriculture has succeeded a wide variety of cereals are raised as well as many varieties of fruits and vegetables. In this connection, it may also be interesting to state that in many sections of the state grain crops are now grown without irrigation.[3] In 1914, about five-sevenths of the wheat grown was on dry farm lands. The irrigation lands being used more and more for the raising of sugar beets, vegetables, and fruits. It is esti-

---

[1]In May 1903 Theodore Roosevelt made a speech in the Salt Lake Tabernacle in which he referred to the development of irrigation in Utah in the following words, as quoted by Orson F. Whitney: 'Irrigation was first practiced on a large scale in this state. The necessity of the pioneers here led to the development of irrigation to a degree absolutely unknown before upon this continent, and in no respect was the wisdom of the early pioneers made more evident than in the sedulous care they took to provide for small farms carefully tilled by those who lived on and benefited from them.' (Whitney, O. F., Popular History of Utah, pp. 549-550.)

[2]In the early period during the fifties and sixties, about 277 canals with a total length of over a thousand miles, and irrigating over 150,000 acres, were constructed. at a cost of upward of $2,000,000. Since that time many more extensive irrigation projects have been carried out of reclaiming the desert lands. For example during the years 1911-1912, $4,000,000 were spent on irrigation projects. (See, Bancroft, H. H., History of Utah, p. 722, and, Young, L. E., Story of Utah, p. 32.)

*The following is an extract from the Report of the State Bureau of Immigration and Statistics: "Utah was the first territory or state to adopt irrigation as a means towards establishing the agricultural industry in the Rocky Mountain States. Since that time, which was in 1847, over $20,000,000, have been expended upon the principal irrigation enterprises, and many more thousands of dollars on smaller individual irrigation systems. Reservoirs to impound water have been built to the number of 500, besides 6000 miles of main canals and 2,000 miles of laterals." (Statistics and Resources of Utah, 1917, p. 19.)

[3]Dr. John A. Widtsoe states: "The honor of having originated modern dry farming belongs to the people of Utah. . . . . About 1860, the first dry-farming experiments of any consequence occurred in Utah." (Widtsoe, J. A., Dry-farming, pp. 354-355.)

mated that more than 1,000,000 acres of dry farm land is under cultivation in Utah.[1]

The land surface of Utah is approximately 52,597,760 acres, and in 1920, of this area, 5,505,410 acres, or 9.6 per cent, of the state's land area was in farms, and 34 per cent of the farm land is improved.[2]

The following tables will show the progress of agriculture in Utah:

STATISTICS OF AGRICULTURE

TABLE I. NUMBER OF FARMS, AND FARM ACREAGE[3*]

Census Year	Farms No.	Per Cent Increase	Acres	Per Cent Increase
1920[4]	25,662	18.4	5,050,410	48.6
1910	21,676	11.8	3,397,699[5]	−17.5 (decrease)
1900	19,387	84.3	4,116,951	211.0
1890	10,517	11.3	1,323,705	101.9
1880	9,452	92.6	655,524	341.8
1870	4,908	35.0	148,361	65.0
1860	3,635	292.5	89,911	91.9
1850	926		46,849	

[1]See Utah Facts and Figures, 1913-14, p. 55.

[2]See Report of the Industrial Commission of Utah, July 1, 1918 to June 30, 1920, p. 317.

[3]Thirteenth Census of the United States, 1910, Supplement for Utah, p. 598.

[*]In 1917, Utah had about 23,000 farms averaging about 150 acres. The improved farms average above 65 acres. Statistics and Resources of Utah, 1917, p. 19.

[4]Report of the Industrial Commission of Utah (Period, July 1, 1918 to June 30, 1920) p. 317.

[5]Although there was a decrease in the acreage of 1910 as compared with the acreage of 1900, there was an increase in improved land. In 1900, there were 1,032,117 acres in improved land, while in 1910, there were 1,368,211 acres.

TABLE II.　VALUE OF FARM PROPERTY: 1850 TO 1920[1]

Census Year	Total		Land and Buildings		Machinery and Implements		Domestic Animals, Poultry and Bees	
	Value	Per Cent of Increase	Value	Per Cent of Increase	Value	Per Cent of Increase	Value	Per Cent of Increase
1920*	$311,275,728	106.4	$243,751,758	107.4	$13,514,787	202.5	$54,008,185	87.6
1910	150,795,201	100.6	117,545,332	131.5	4,468,178	52.9	28,781,691	34.0
1900	75,175,141	90.4	50,778,350	78.8	2,922,550	150.9	21,474,241	116.6
1890	39,482,206	104.2	28,402,780	102.7	1,164,660	23.0	9,914,766	126.8
1880	19,333,569	409.9	14,015,176	662.4	946,753	306.1	4,371,638	154.2
1870	3,791,301	22.6	1,838,338	37.9	233,112	-4.0	1,719,851	13.4
1860	3,092,951	228.0	1,333,353	327.6	242,889	188.2	1,516,707	177.3
1850	943,055		311,799		84,288		546,968	

[1]Thirteenth Census of the United States, 1910, Supplement for Utah, p. 598.
*Fourteenth Census of the United States, 1920, Advanced Bulletin, Agriculture—Utah, p. 3.

Farm and Livestock Products.—The value of the principal farm and livestock products for the year 1909 was $28,984,701.[1]

The value of farm products in 1917 was about $40,000,000 and the returns from the livestock industry, for animals sold and slaughtered, and for wool clipped and sold was around $15,000,000.[2]

The aggregate value of the crops of Utah in 1919 was $57,980,827.

The total number of cattle in Utah in 1919 was 505,578, and their estimated value was reported as $22,627,870.

The value of all dairy products was $4,409,087, and the value of poultry products, $2,887,571.[3]

Farm Tenure.—The amount of farm tenure in Utah has thus far been small. In 1920, 88 per cent of all the farms were operated by the owners, while in 1910, 91.2 per cent were operated by the owners.[4]

(2) FORESTS

The lumber industry has never assumed any particular importance in the industrial development of the state. While there is a fair supply of common timber for ordinary use, there is a scarcity of the better grades of hard woods.

The total wooded area is about 10,000 square miles, which is about 12.5 per cent of the land area of the state.[5]

(3) MANUFACTURING

While agriculture and mining are the chief occupations carried on in the state, there has also been, in recent years, a rapid development of manufacturing. The water of the numerous streams has been utilized to generate electrical energy to be used in manufacturing, mining, transportation and other industries.

The growth of the mining industry and the cultivation of sugar beets as well as the expansion of transportation facilities have contributed to the growth of manufacturing.

[1]Thirteenth Census of the United States, 1910, Vol. 7, Agriculture, pp. 715-728.
[2]Statistics and Resources of Utah, 1917. p. 19.
[3]Report of the Industrial Commission of Utah, July 1, 1918 to June 30, 1920, p. 318.
[4]Thirteenth Census of the United States, 1910, Vol. 7, Agriculture, p. 718, and Fourteenth Census of the United States, 1920, (Agriculture—Utah (Advanced Bulletin), p. 4.
[5]Bancroft, H. H., History of Utah, p. 727.

In 1849, there were fourteen manufacturing establishments which gave employment to about fifty wage-earners. By 1880, upward of 2,500 persons were employed, and Bancroft reports that there were at this time, "at least 75 flour and grist mills, 100 lumber mills, 18 furniture factories, 20 boot and shoe factories, and 7 foundaries and machine shops.[1] By 1909, the number of manufacturing establishments had increased to 749, and 14, 133 persons were employed[2]. In 1919 there were 1,160 manufacturing establishments and 23.107 persons were employed.[3]

In 1850, the value of manufactured products amounted to about $300,000. By 1880, the value had increased to about $5,000,000, and since that time there has been a continuous increase each year until 1919, when the total value of the manufactured products reached approximately $156,933,071.[4]

The capital employed in manufactures likewise, has greatly increased. In 1899 the amount of capital invested in manufacturing concerns, was about $13,219,039, in 1904, $26,004,011, in 1909, $52,626,640, and in 1919, $140,785,034.[5]

The leading manufacturing industries are lead and copper smelting, milling of flour, manufacture of beet sugar, railroad car-repairing, dairying, canning, meat-packing, and confectionery industries.[6]

(4) MINING

The mineral resources of Utah are varied and valuable, and quite generally distributed throughout the state. The mountains contain gold, silver, lead, copper, iron, and coal. Building stone is also plentiful and is found in great variety, and the mountains and Great Salt Lake contain almost an inexhaustible supply of salt. It has been pointed out by Professor Young that iron mines were developed in Utah as early as 1852.[7] The mining industry, however, did not begin to any great extent until the early sixties.

Whitney in his history of Utah describes the growth of the

[1]Bancroft, H. H., History of Utah, p. 733.
[2]Thirteenth Census of the United States, Vol. 9, Manufacturing, p. 1225.
[3]Fourteenth Census of the United States, Manufactures, 1919, Utah, (Advanced Bulletin), p. 4.
[4]Fourteenth Census of the United States, Manufacturies, 1919—Utah, (Advanced Bulletin), p. 4.
[5]Ibid., p. 4.
[6]For a further summary of the growth of manufacturing in Utah, see Deseret Evening News, December 20, 1920.
[7]Young, L. E., Story of Utah, p. 16.

mining industry in the following words: "From 1861 until 1865, mining in Utah was an infant in arms. From 1870, it was a youth, strong and vigorous, and ten years later developed into marvelous manhood. To-day it is great and still growing."[1]

Bancroft in his work on Utah has also showed the development of mining in this state. He points out that, "for 1869 the product of all the Utah mines in gold, silver, and lead did not exceed $200,000. In 1871, it had risen to $3,000,000, and in 1875, to $7,000,000 . . . . . . Between 1870 and 1883 there were produced $2,150,000 in gold, $45,790,272 in silver, 258,000 tons of lead, worth at the Atlantic seaboard $23,220,000, and 1,000 tons of copper which sold in New York for about $300,000. The total output for this period was $71,502,772. At the close of 1883, there were at least 95 districts in Utah where mining of various descriptions was in progress, all of them contributing more or less to the total yield, though the great volume of production was confined to the few."[2]

In 1915, the metal output aggregated in value $61,081,633,[3] and again it may be added that the known metal products of the state up to 1915, (gold, silver, copper, lead, zinc), have been valued at $727,558,498.[4]

In 1919 Utah ranked eighteenth among the states in value of mineral products. The amount received for products of all mines and quarries in 1919 was $41,510,802.[5]

In 1919 the mines and quarries employed 9,847 wage-earners.[6]

6. TRANSPORTATION AND COMMERCE

(1) TRANSPORTATION

Transportation has always been a significant factor in the history of the Far West. The early settlers of Utah felt the need of good transportation facilities and, therefore, encouraged road-making and bridge-building.

In 1869, the transcontinental railroad was completed[7] and

---

[1]Whitney, O. F., Popular History of Utah, C. 26, p. 561.
[2]Bancroft, H. H., History of Utah, p. 747.
[3]Whitney, O. F., Popular History of Utah, C. 26.
[4]Report of the State Bureau of Immigration, Labor and Statistics, 1917, p. 18.
[5]Fourteenth Census of the United States, Mines and Quarries, (Idaho, Nevada, Utah), 1919, (Advanced Bulletin), p. 11.
[6]Ibid., p. 12.
[7]In 1869, the Union Pacific and the Central Pacific Railroads were united at Promontory Point, Utah.

Utah was given access to the markets of the Mississippi Valley and the Pacific Coast. Since that date the railroad system of this intermountain region has been supplemented by various branch lines made to districts of the state which have grown into arteries of commerce.

In 1870, there were about 270 miles of railroad in Utah. By 1883, there were 1,143 miles, and by 1895, there were over 1800 miles. The state now has over 2,350 miles of railroad.[1]

The trans-continental telegraph was also finished in 1862 and Utah by this means, as well as by the railroads, was brought in touch with other sections of our country.

(2) TRADE AND COMMERCE

The progress and development of trade and commerce in Utah from 1848 to the present time seems rather phenomenal, especially when we consider that the entire cash capital in Salt Lake City in 1848 did not in all probability exceed $3,000.

During the early period of money scarcity, exchange and barter was the rule. Merchants exchanged their groceries and dry-goods for the products of the farm, the mill, and the workshop. The first settlers also made and used substitute paper money until the coins of our national government became sufficiently plentiful.

In the early days, the manufactured goods were brought principally from California and Saint Louis.[2] By 1864, however, several firms[3] in Salt Lake City were purchasing goods in New York City, Chicago, and Saint Louis to the value of about $250,000, or more at a time.

With the coming of the railroad, an impetus was given to trade and industrialism in general. The population increased and much more capital came into the territory. The mining industry was greatly developed and there was a general expansion of the manufacturing industries. The domestic imports and exports greatly increased. By 1882, for example, the imports amounted to over $11,000,000 and the exports to about $11,500,000. The imports consisted largely of dry-goods, gro-

[1]See Bancroft, H. H., History of Utah, p. 752, and, The World Book, Vol. 8, p. 6014.

[2]Kinkead and Livingston, a Saint Louis firm, brought a large stock of merchandise across the plains in the fall of 1849.

[3]One of the oldest and largest firms in Utah is that knows as "Zions Cooperative Mercantile Institution". This commercial enterprise now has an annual trade of over $6,000,000.

ceries, leather, agricultural implements, etc., and the exports, principally of metals, gold, silver, lead, and also live stock, beef, and wool.[1]

At the present time, the state is assuming a position of importance in the way of a financial and industrial center in the intermountain region. In 1909 the value of manufactured products was $61,989,277, and in 1919 the value of the products amounted to $156,933,071.[2]

To-day in Utah there are also about 112 banking concerns. Of this number, 22 are national banks,[3] about 75 are state banks, and some 15 private banks, as well as a few loan and trust companies. The national banks have a capital of $3,500,000 and a surplus of $1,600,000, and deposits aggregating $22,000,000. The capital of the 75 state banks is about $4,500,000 with a surplus of about $1,100,000, and deposits aggregating $23,000,000.

The assessed valuation of property in Utah in 1919, was about $540,500,000.[4]

7. OCCUPATION STATISTICS

TABLE I. CLASSIFICATION BY AGES OF THE GAINFULLY EMPLOYED IN 1910.[5]

Age Periods	Males			Females		
	Total Number	Number Employed	Per Cent	Total Number	Number Employed	Per Cent
Population 10 years of age and over..	147,009	113,113	76.9	127,769	18,427	14.4
10 to 13 years	16,367	1,040	6.4	15,834	90	0.6
14 to 15 years	7,530	1,771	23.5	7,572	330	4.4
16 to 20 years	18,997	13,194	69.5	18,634	4,752	25.5
21 to 44 years	74,025	70,642	95.4	59,468	10,250	17.2
45 years and over	30,090	26,466	88.0	26,261	3,005	11.4

[1]Bancroft, H. H., History of Utah, p. 762.

[2]Fourteenth Census of the United States, 1920, Manufacturers: Utah, (Advanced Bulletin), p. 4.

[3]The first national bank was established in 1872, and a year later, savings banks began their activities.

[4]For a more complete account of Utah's resources, see, the Report of the Bureau of Immigration, Labor and Statistics, 1917, pp. 18-23.

[5]Thirteenth Census of the United States, 1910, Vol. V, Occupations, p. 73.

TABLE II.   TOTAL PERSONS 10 YEARS OF AGE AND OVER
ENGAGED IN SPECIFIED OCCUPATIONS.   CLASSIFIED
BY SEX, 1910[1]

Occupation	Male		Female	
	Number	Per Cent Distribution	Number	Per Cent Distribution
All occupations............................	113,113	100	18,427	100
1. Agriculture, forestry and animal husbandry...............	36,500	32.3	917	5.0
2. Extraction of minerals.....	10,014	8.9	5	*
3. Manufacturing and mechanical industries...............	27,783	24.6	3,360	18.2
4. Transportation	11,828	10.5	494	2.7
5. Trade.................	11,187	9.8	1,892	10.3
6. Public service......................	2,370	2.1	150	0.8
7. Professional service.............	4,783	4.2	3,099	16.8
8. Domestic and personal service............................	4,353	3.8	6,497	35.3
9. Clerical occupations.............	4,395	3.8	2,103	10.9

No printed bulletin or report has yet been issued of occupations from 1920 census returns. Preliminary press announcements, however, have been issued for states and for cities, having 25,000 inhabitants or more. A letter from W. M. Stewart, Director of the United States Census Bureau, March 2, 1922, contains the following preliminary occupation statistics for Utah, and the general occupation statistics of Ogden and Salt Lake City.

According to the report of Mr. Steward there were, in 1920, 331,530 persons 10 years of age and over in Utah. Of this number 149,201 or 45 per cent were engaged in gainful occupations. The total male population 10 years of age and over was 172,295, and of this number 127,417 or 74 per cent were gainfully employed. The total female population 10 years of age and over was 159,235 and of this number 21,784 or 13.7 per cent were engaged in gainful occupations.

Of the males gainfully occupied 42,372 were engaged in agriculture, forestry, and animal husbandry; 10,096 in the extraction of minerals; 30,916 in manufacturing and mechanical industries; 11,484 in transportation; 13,528 in trade; 2,285 in public service; 5,668 in professional service; 4,713 in domestic and personal service; and 6,355 in clerical occupations. Of the females occupied, 887 were engaged in agriculture, forestry, and animal husbandry; 21 in the extraction of minerals; 2,680 in manufacturing and mechanical industries; 945 in transportation; 3,015 in trade; 183 in public service; 4,329 in professional service; 5,457 in domestic and personal service; and 4,267 in clerical occupations.

[1]Thirteenth Census of the United States, 1910, Vol. 4, Occupation Statistics, pp. 46-49.
*Less than one-tenth of one per cent.

TABLE III. PRINCIPAL OCCUPATIONS FOLLOWED BY MALES AND FEMALES RESPECTIVELY IN UTAH IN 1920 AND 1910[1]

OCCUPATION	Male		Female	
	1920	1910	1920	1910
All occupations	127,417	113,113	21,784	18,427
Agents, canvassers, and collectors	810	532	51	32
Bankers, brokers, and money lenders	680	468	26	12
Barbers, hairdressers, and manicurists	715	617	84	98
Blacksmiths, forgemen, and hammermen	1,036	1,108	–	–
Bookkeepers, cashiers, and accountants	1,935	1,349	1,119	581
Carpenters	3,519	3,765	1	–
Civil engineers and surveyors	501	498	–	–
Clergymen	205	284	2	–
Clerks, except clerks in store	2,953	1,803	865	318
Clerks in stores	576	1,037	580	680
Coal-mine operatives	3,725	2,318	6	–
Commercial travelers	721	607	10	15
Copper-mine operatives	1,564	1,632	–	–
Draymen, teamsters, and expressmen	1,457	1,804	2	–
Dressmakers, and seamstresses, not in factories	–	4	759	1,587
Electricians and electrical engineers	1,165	904	–	–
Engineers, stationary	863	924	2	–
Farmers, general farms	22,298	17,437	536	453
Farm laborers (home farm)	4,870	5,827	96	141
Farm laborers (working out)	9,786	7,722	108	100
Foremen and overseers, manufacturing	743	314	41	29
Gardeners, florists, fruitgrowers, and nurserymen	674	754	33	42
Gold-and silver-mine operatives	2,920	2,978	1	2
Housekeepers and stewards	50	25	637	464
Janitors and sextons	748	394	147	96
Laborers, building, general, and not specified	3,260	5,824	40	81
Laborers, copper factories	1,451	1,399	1	8
Laborers, steam railroad	2,480	4,188	48	12
Laborers, sugar factories and refineries	1,186	189	51	1
Lawyers, judges, and justices	526	444	1	2
Locomotive engineers	739	734	–	–
Locomotive firemen	575	499	–	–
Machinists, millwrights, and toolmakers	2,010	1,120	–	–
Managers and superintendents, manufacturing	729	327	10	3
Midwives and nurses (not trained)	38	36	657	643
Mining engineers	288	302	–	–
Musicians and teachers of music	317	351	317	412
Painters, glaziers, and varnishers, building	844	890	1	1
Physicians and surgeons	481	439	22	55
Plumbers and gas and steam fitters	732	544	–	–
Real-estate agents and officials	486	542	49	11
Retail dealers	4,423	3,956	223	198
Salesmen and saleswomen	3,886	2,323	2,059	935
Servants and waiters	1,463	1,255	2,450	3,173
Stenographers and typewriters	288	322	2,183	1,059
Stock herders, drovers, and feeders	2,115	2,207	7	24
Stock raisers	1,272	1,350	10	19
Teachers, school	1,042	841	2,894	2,050
Trained nurses	12	15	544	225

TABLE IV. PRELIMINARY OCCUPATION STATISTICS OF THE TWO
PRINCIPAL CITIES OF UTAH—OGDEN AND SALT
LAKE CITY, IN 1920[1]

Occupations	Ogden		Salt Lake City	
	Number	Per Cent Distribution	Number	Per Cent Distribution
Gainful workers 10 years of age and over	11,790	100	45,894	100
Manufacturing and mechanical industries	3,756	31.9	12,808	27.9
Transportation	1,936	16.4	5,070	11.0
Trade	1,978	16.8	8,366	18.2
Public service	218	1.8	1,292	2.8
Professional service	854	7.2	4,454	9.7
Domestic and professional service	1,108	9.4	4,930	10.7
Clerical occupations	1,465	12.4	6,538	14.2
All other occupations	475	4.0	2,436	5.3

The 11,790 persons 10 years of age and over in Ogden, engaged in gainful occupations in 1920, constituted 35.9 per cent of the total population of the city (32,804) and 46.4 per cent of the population 10 years of age and over. In 1910 the 9,380 gainful workers were 36.7 per cent of the total population of the city and 47.2 per cent of the population 10 years of age and over.

Of the gainful workers of Ogden in 1920, 9,528 or 80.8 per cent, were males and 2,262, or 19.2 per cent, were females. The male gainful workers constituted 74.8 per cent of all males 10 years of age and over in 1920, as against 73.9 per cent in 1910, while the female gainful workers constituted 17.9 per cent of all females 10 years of age and over in 1920, as against 17.7 per cent in 1910.

The 45,894 persons 10 years of age and over in Salt Lake City, engaged in gainful occupations in 1920, constituted 38.9 per cent of the total population of the city (118,110) and 49.2 per cent of population 10 years of age and over. In 1910 the 37,730 gainful workers were 40.7 per cent of the total population of the city and 51.3 per cent of the population 10 years of age and over.

[1]The above preliminary general occupation statistics issued by the Department of Commerce from the Bureau of the Census, which, though subject to change, are approximately correct.

Of the gainful workers of Salt Lake in 1920, 35,802, or 78.0 per cent were males and 10,092, or 22.0 per cent, were females. The male gainful workers constituted 77.7 per cent of all males 10 years of age and over in 1920, as against 79.9 per cent in 1910, while the female gainful workers constituted 21.5 per cent of all females 10 years of age and over in 1920, as against 20.9 per cent in 1910.

PART II
TERRITORIAL PERIOD
1850-1896

CHAPTER II

THE LABOR LEGISLATION OF THE TERRITORIAL PERIOD

Very little labor legislation was enacted in Utah during the territorial period. The population was small and the people for the most part were engaged in agricultural pursuits.[1]

Outside of the farming population living in small towns and villages, and operating their own farms, there was indeed only a small group which might be classed as wage-earners, that is, people dependent upon their daily wages for their support. In the main, therefore, we may look upon this period as marking the beginning of industrial life in this district, a matter which was described in some detail in the introductory chapter to this study.

A number of labor measures, however, were passed by the territorial legislatures and we will review them here in the order in which they were enacted. They show the trend that labor legislation took in the early period in Utah as well as serving as a supplement to our main treatise, that is, labor legislation during the period of statehood.

1. CHILD WELFARE LEGISLATION

The Act of 1852.—The first labor enactment in Utah was an act passed in 1852,[2] concerning masters and apprentices.

This measure was very limited in its application for it referred only to minors who served as apprentices.

The binding out during minority was to be done by written indenture, and when the minor was over twelve years of age he was to sign the agreement.

The master was required to send the apprentice to school,

---

[1] Generally speaking labor legislation in this country has had little to do with farm labor. (See Commons, J. R., and Andrews, J. B., Principles of Labor Legislation, Rev. ed. 1920, p. 62.

[2] Utah, Laws 1852, C. 162.

between the ages of six and sixteen, for a period of three months in each school year, if there was a school in the district or vicinity, and to clothe the minor child, and otherwise discharge his duties as specified in the indenture.

The parent, or guardian, or officer by whose act the minor was thus bound was required to watch over the apprentice and take measures for his or her relief when circumstances justified such action, that is, if the master ill-treated the minor child, or otherwise failed to discharge his duties toward the apprentice. In his event, the minor so bound might be discharged from further service, and compensation for services and damages might be recovered.

The indenture was dissolved or cancelled by the death of the master, or his removal from the territory, unless otherwise provided for in the indenture; or unless the apprentice elected to continue in his service.

The early lawmakers regarded the apprenticeship system largely in the light of a convenient means of caring for dependent or incorrigible children. The selectmen, or the probate courts, were given the right to bind out incorrigible, or vagrant children without their consent or the consent of their parents, if such parents refused or neglected to control the actions and education of such minors.

This measure certainly did not go far in the regulation of the employment of children, as its nature would imply, but it has importance largely in the sense that it marks the beginning of legislation in the interest of children in the territory.

This apprenticeship statute,[1] in a way, reflected the apprenticeship system which was common in the United States until after the Civil War, when as we know, modern industry greatly developed and made imperative restrictive child labor laws.

Early School Laws.—The school laws figure in our treatise only as they may throw light on our main theme of labor legislation. In a subsequent chapter, however, we will have occasion to show how they supplement the child labor laws and serve as a potent factor in mitigating child labor. In passing, however,

---

[1]In this connection, it is well to add that the early inhabitants of Utah were men and women who had formerly lived in New England and in the Middle Atlantic States, as well as immigrants from northern Europe, chiefly from England who were familiar with the apprenticeship system. Their knowledge of apprenticeship laws elsewhere influenced this piece of legislation.

it may be well to refer briefly to the establishment of schools in the territory.[1]

In 1854[2] a measure was passed by the legislature relating to common or public schools in the territory.

Since this time various school laws have been enacted, extending and supplementing the earlier educational measures.

School officials, trustees and superintendents were given jurisdiction over school matters in their respective districts. They determined from the revenue available for school purposes, the length of the school term. The early enactments did not require compulsory attendance on the part of the school children, but in 1890,[3] a school law was passed which, among other things, made provision for compulsory attendance. Children between ten and fourteen years of age were required to attend school at least sixteen weeks of every school year, unless legally excused by school officials.

It seems evident that the early law requiring compulsory attendance was seldom rigorously enforced by school officials, but yet it undoubtedly worked for the ultimate good of children. In certain cases, no doubt, children remained in school for a longer period than would otherwise have been the case.

2. BUREAU OF STATISTICS

At this point it may also be well to mention the beginning of a Bureau of Statistics in the territory. In 1874,[4] the legislature established a Bureau of Statistics in connection with and under the direction of the Deseret Agricultural and Manufacturing Society which took cognizance of the material interests of Utah.

In 1892,[5] the territorial librarian was made territorial statistician. This bureau, however, during this early period, had little to do with the question of labor, but we mention the establishment of the bureau here, because later, in the period of

[1]The settlers of Utah believed in education, and early established schools. In 1850, the legislature made provisions for the establishment of a university, said to be the first university west of the Missouri River. (See, Legislative Assembly; Acts, Resolutions, and Memorials; 1850, C. 2, and Young, L. E., Story of Utah, p. 22.)
[2]Utah, Laws 1850-1870, C. 94.
[3]Utah, Laws 1890, C. 72.
[4]Utah, Laws 1874, C. 21.
[5]Utah, Laws 1892, C. 46.

statehood, it developed into the Bureau of Labor, of whose activities we shall have occasion to speak in a later chapter.

3. SAFETY AND HEALTH

The relatively simple economic conditions of life in Utah during the territorial period did not give rise to a great deal of legislation looking to the safety and health of workers. Not until the period of statehood do we find any considerable development of safety legislation.

The first need for legislation of this nature was in connection with the mining industry, and principally in connection with coal mines. Accidents happening from time to time prompted the enactment of protective measures in this hazardous occupation.

In 1880,[1] a very general act was passed concerning the sinking of shafts for ventilating mines. These shafts were to be enclosed with a fence or curb to prevent persons or animals from falling into them. Violation of the act made the offender liable to damages.

Some twelve years later several much more elaborate provisions were enacted into law looking to the safety of miners working in coal mines. The first act of 1892[2] looked to the means of providing exits, or escapement shafts in coal mines. The law required that all coal mines where ten or more men were employed should be provided with escapement shafts, or tunnels. The act also stipulated that violators were subject to a fine of not more than $1000, or imprisonment for one year, or both, in the discretion of the court for each and every offence.

The second law[3] passed this same year, 1892, by the legislature was concerned with the supply and placing of timbers in coal mines. Owners or operators of coal mines were required to keep on hand and use props or timbers to properly secure the workings from caving in. These timbers were to be placed not more than 300 feet from the face of such workings.

Violation of the act carried with it the same punishment as described in the first act mentioned above.

These acts, however, did not make provisions for their enforcement. In the absence, therefore, of any special official

[1] Utah, Laws 1880, C. 35.
[2] Utah, Laws 1892, C. 38.
[3] Utah, Laws 1892, C. 41.

entrusted with the administration of the laws, they were enforced by local officials in a rather desultory manner.

4. LAWS FOR THE PROTECTION OF THE WAGES OF LABOR

A mechanic's lien law was enacted in 1890[1] to give protection to wage-workers. In this first effort, however, to render more secure the payment of the wages of labor, the law merely pointed out who might secure liens. Material-men, those furnishing material as well as laborers doing work of any kind, were given the right to secure liens on buildings.

At the next session of the legislature in 1892 a law[2] was passed making wages the preferred claim in the division of the proceeds of the seizure or transfer of property, or funds available for the satisfaction of liens.

When the property of any firm or corporation was suspended by the action of creditors or seized upon by process of any court in the territory, debts owing laborers and servants were to be treated as preferred debts. This might apply to all labor performed within six months prior to the seizure or transfer of such property. In cases, however, where there was not sufficient funds to pay laborers in full they were to be paid in proportion to the amount due them.

Certain provisions in the law also referred to the manner of enforcement of claims. Statements by claimants under oath, were to be made showing the amount of wages due them, the kind of work performed, and the like.

In 1894,[3] the earlier mechanics lien law of 1890 was repealed, and a new measure was enacted to allow mechanics, builders, and laborers of every class rendering service, as well as material-men, to attach liens on the property on which they performed labor. The lien included buildings, bridges, tunnels, and the like. No liens, however, were to attach to public buildings.

In all probability this legislation was first prompted by material-men-claimants furnishing material for the construction or repair of buildings, bridges, etc. Yet, these measure seem to show that the purpose legislators had in mind in enacting these laws was to protect the rights of the laborer as well as the material-man.

[1]Utah, Laws 1890, C. 30.
[2]Utah, Laws 1892, C. 30.
[3]Utah, Laws 1894, C. 41.

In Part III, of this study, we shall have occasion to trace the further development of legislation of this nature, and to show more substantial progress in the protection of the wages of laborers.

5. HOURS OF LABOR

Only a beginning was made in the territorial period to regulate hours of labor. A law was enacted in 1894,[1] just prior to statehood, establishing an eight-hour day on public works. The term "public works" included all works belonging to or paid for by the territory or any political subdivision thereof.

[1]Utah, Laws 1894, C. 11.

PART III
PERIOD OF STATEHOOD
1896-1921

CHAPTER III

LEGISLATION CONCERNING THE EMPLOYMENT OF CHILDREN

Children in Utah in the territorial period were not to any great extent engaged in industrial life as wage-earners. They worked for the most part with their parents as helpers and learners, and where home conditions were satisfactory such labor was perhaps not harmful to their physical or moral well-being.

In recent years, however, with the growth of various industries in the state the tendency has been for more young people to become gainfully employed in enterprises other than those owned or operated by their parents. In view of this fact, measures have been enacted looking to the welfare and protection of young, immature, wage-earners.

These child labor laws have been based for the most part on the consideration of the age, health, and education of children. It has also been found expedient to make these enactments of both a direct and indirect nature, that is, indirect acts prohibiting or restricting the employment of children and in direct measures supplementing the legal restrictions by setting forth certain educational requirements before children are allowed to become gainfully employed.

1. EXTENT OF CHILD LABOR

It was pointed out in the opening chapter[1] that in 1910 there were 3,231 children[2] from 10 to 15 years of age engaged in some form of gainful work. Of this number, 2,811 were boys and 420 were girls; or otherwise stated the total number of children employed was about 11.8 per cent of the males, and about 1.8 per cent of the females, 10 to 15 years of age.[3]

[1]See C. 1, pp. 24-28.

[2]The total number of gainful workers for the two age periods, 10 to 13 and 14 to 15 years, as set forth in Chapter I, Table I, p. 24, equals the number of children mentioned above.

[3]According to the Federal Census of 1910, the number of children of each sex, 10 to 15 years of age, engaged in gainful occupations in the U. S. was as follows: male 24.8 per cent; female 11.9 per cent. (Thirteenth Census of U. S. 1910, Vol. 4, p. 70.)

Of the total number of males and females 10 to 15 years of age engaged as gainful workers in 1910 nearly 2,100 of the boys were employed in agricultural work, and about 200 girls were employed in domestic and personal service. About 100 boys were employed in manufacturing and mechanical industries and a similar number in trade as classified by the census report. Various miscellaneous occupations connected with domestic and personal service, clerical work, etc., included the majority of the boy workers not represented in the selected occupations mentioned above. For the girls, outside of the domestic and personal service, a small number were engaged in clerical service and as helpers on dairy and fruit farms. Less than a dozen of the girls were listed in the Federal Census as being engaged in manufacturing and mechanical industries.[1]

These figures show conditions before any very far reaching legislation was enacted in the state looking to the regulation of the employment of children. Since 1910, a number of child labor laws have been passed which practically prohibit child labor in the state in so far as industrial work is concerned. The child labor which exists is largely in connection with agriculture and domestic service and the work of newsboys and boot-blacks in the urban districts. Again, we may add that where the tendency has been for young people to become gainful workers the cases refer usually to young wage-earners over fourteen years of age.

2. CAUSES OF CHILD LABOR

Child labor wherever found has usually been attributed to four or five principal causes, viz: (1) where their earnings are regarded as necessary for the support of the family; (2) machine technique which enables children to perform the simpler processes in industry; (3) efforts of many employers to obtain cheap labor; (4) failure of the schools to hold the attention and arouse the ambition of the restless youth; (5) indifference on the part of the public to conditions as they exist and to the ultimate effects that the entrance of young children into industry must have on society in general. Doubtless all these causes have contributed to child labor in Utah.

The data obtainable, however, relating to the extent of child labor in this state show quite conclusively that very little child

[1]Thirteenth Census of U. S. 1910, Vol. 4, p. 523.

labor is found and where it does exist, it is largely in connection with agriculture and domestic service—occupations which are not usually regarded as hazardous or particularly harmful to children if their employment is wisely supervised. We may also state that the work on the farms usually lasts but for a short period during the summer months when children are not in attendance at school.

From our knowledge of conditions in this state it seems that the cases of gainfully employed children on farms are not due in any great measure to extreme poverty in their home life, but are due rather to a desire on the part of these children fourteen to sixteen years of age to earn their own money, and thus supply their wants more freely than their parents are able or disposed to do. On the other hand, in certain cases, the earnings of young members of the household are. necessary to supplement the family income.

Farmers often experience difficulty, during the harvest season, in securing the services of a sufficient number of workmen to help them garner their crops, so frequently children aid in such work. On the other hand, it would be difficult to find many farmers who regard the employment of children as very profitable to them.

In the urban sections of the state the first cause given, the necessity for the earnings of young members of the household for the support of the family, probably figures more in the employment of children than in the rural districts. Misfortune, ill-health, or the death of the bread winner of a family may account in certain cases for placing the responsibility of providing the necessities of life prematurely upon the young members of the household. Again, shirking of responsibility by the head of the household to supply the family with those things necessary to make home life happy and attractive may also operate to cause boys and girls to seek gainful employment.

3. PROMOTION OF CHILD LABOR LAWS

The people quite generally recognize the unsoundness, from the standpoint of the physical well-being of children, of permitting their entrance into industry at an early age in life; and especially early entrance into mines, mills, or factories.

Legislation of this character in the interest of children, however, has been influenced by the growth of the state public educational system. The people have always manifested an interest in education and at a very early period in their history, as has been pointed out, they gave attention to this question. Furthermore, many ambitious parents have been desirous of giving their children extended educational advantages beyond the legal requirements set forth in the school law.

In addition to the schools serving as a substitute for the factory and workshop, we may also account for the small utilization of child labor in gainful occupations by the rather favorable economic condition of many of the people in this state. Only in rare instances are young children ten, twelve, or fourteen years of age required to contribute to their own support. The work they do consists in the main of the lighter tasks which usually fall to boys and girls about the home.

In this connection also we must not fail to mention that the industrial life of the state has not given rise to a great demand for the continuous and extended use of child labor. Agriculture is still the dominant occupation of the people of the state.

The child labor laws have generally been the outcome of sentiment crystallized by women's clubs and labor organizations. These agencies as well as the State Bureau of Labor, have been most active in the promotion and upholding of labor laws.

Again, the general interest given to the question of child labor during the last decade or so, in this country especially in connection with the work of the National Child Labor Committee has likewise influenced public opinion in Utah to raise the standard for the entrance of children into industry.

4. CHILD LABOR LEGISLATION

The State Constitution adopted in 1896 made it mandatory upon the legislature to prohibit "the employment of women, or of children under the age of fourteen years, in underground mines."[1]

In conformity with this requirement, as set forth in the State Constitution, the legislature passed an act in 1896,[2] prohibiting the employment of any female, or child under the age of fourteen years in any mine or smelter in the state.

Mining and smelting industries were regarded as extra hazardous occupations more susceptible to danger than agriculture or many other kinds of employment which children enter; and,

[1] Utah, State Constitution, Art. 16, Sec. 3.
[2] Utah, Laws 1896, C. 28.

therefore, a minimum age requirement was set for entrance into these industries.

This, generally speaking, marks the beginning of prohibitive legislation for children in Utah. From this time onward, the legislature has, at various sessions, passed measures relative to the employment of children. The child labor laws also have been enlarged and amended from time to time as conditions seem to warrant such expansion.

We regard the child labor law passed by the state legislature in 1911[1] as the foundation for the more recent measures looking to the welfare of children. In fact the progress made in child labor legislation in the state since this law was enacted has been largely by way of amendments to this basic measure, which because of its importance is presented in some detail.

(1) ACT OF 1911

The gist of the act of 1911 is as follows:

Age Limit: No child under the age of fourteen years shall be employed in any of the following industries:

(a) In establishments where dangerous or poisonous acids are prepared or used;

(b) Where explosives, tobacco, liquors, or goods for immoral purposes are manufactured;

(c) In quarries, mines, laundries, cigar stores, theatres, concert halls, bowling alleys, pool halls, or saloons;

(d) In connection with the operation of automobiles, motors, trucks, or the management of elevators, or hoisting machines;

(e) In any other employment declared by the State Board of Health as dangerous or injurious to the child's life, limb, health and morals.

Other Occupations Forbidden.—The act further provides for different age requirements in employment other than those already enumerated: (a) females under twenty-one years of age are prohibited from working in restaurants, or places of amusement where liquors are manufactured or dispensed; (b) in connection with messenger service in cities of the first or second class, persons under the age of twenty-one are prohibited from delivering goods or messages before five o'clock in the morning, or after nine o'clock in the evening of the same day; (c) no boy under the age of twelve years, or girl under the age of sixteen

[1]Utah, Laws 1911, C. 144.

years is permitted to sell newspapers, magazines, etc., in cities of the first or second class; (d) no child under twelve years of age is allowed to work as a boot-black.

Exceptions, Permits and Employment Certificates.—The exceptions relate to cases where boys under sixteen years of age receive permits to sell newspapers or to work as boot-blacks. These permits are issued by the superintendent of schools according to the following conditions: (a) on application of the parent or guardian of the child desiring the permit; (b) where the boy is twelve years of age and upwards; (c) when the principal of the school where the child is in attendance certifies that the child is physically fit for such employment, and approves of granting such permit; (d) the law provides that a boy receiving a permit must not offer for sale newspapers, magazines, etc., or work as a boot-black, after nine o'clock in the evening.

An employment certificate is issued by the superintendent of schools, but no such certificate is issued until the child in question appears before him, nor until he approves of the school record of such child. The school record signed by the principal of the school which such child has attended must show that the child has ability to read and write the English language, and that the child has attended the public schools for not less than one hundred days during the year previous to his arriving at the age of fourteen years, or during the year previous to the time the working papers are issued.

The employer in permissible occupations is required to furnish to the inspector or truant officer satisfactory evidence of age for any child apparently under fourteen years, that such child is in fact over fourteen years of age.

Hours of Labor.—In addition to fixing an age limit for the employment of children in industry the act also provides for the regulation of the hours of labor for this group. A fifty-hour maximum week was established for boys under fourteen in employments where permitted (street trade, etc.,) and girls under sixteen years of age, except in domestic service, fruit and vegetable packing, and work on farms.

Penalty.—Violation of the act is punishable by a fine of from twenty-five to two hundred dollars, or imprisonment not to exceed thirty days nor less than ten days, or both fine and imprisonment, in the discretion of the court.

Administration.—The law states that any authorized inspector or truant officer shall make demand on any employer in whose establishment a child apparently under the age of fourteen years is employed to give satisfactory evidence that such child is over fourteen years of age or cease to employ such child. Failure to produce within ten days, after demand is made pursuant to this act, the evidence of age herein required shall be prima facie evidence of the illegal employment of such child in any prosecution brought therefor.

No further statement appears in the law as to the duties and powers of inspectors or truant officers except to say that Juvenile courts are given jurisdiction in cases arising under this measure.

In 1915[1], an amendment was made to the child labor law of 1911, making a minor change in regard to employments prohibited to children. In 1917[2], another amendment was passed increasing the prohibitive age limit for the employment of children from fourteen to sixteen years of age in such industries as were enumerated in the basic act of 1911. In employments where permitted (street trades, etc.,) boys under fourteen and girls under sixteen years of age were given an eight-hour day and a forty-eight hour week except in domestic service, fruit, and vegetable packing, and work on farms.

The last amendment to the basic measure of 1911 was passed in 1919.[3] This amendment related to the enforcement of laws governing the employment of children. The administration of the child labor laws was vested in the Industrial Commission of the state.[4]

(2) WAGES

When we turn our attention to the question of wages of children we find that this matter is dealt with in legislation relating to women workers.

The minimum wage law, passed in 1913[5] and treated more fully in Chapter IV, included only female workers. The minimum wage rate was seventy-five cents a day for girls under eighteen.

[1]Utah, Laws 1915, C. 61.
[2]Utah, Laws 1917, C. 80.
[3]Utah, Laws 1919, C. 35.
[4]The Industrial Commission is the agency which now enforces the labor laws of the state. Its powers are given in Chapter VI. It may be well to mention here that a woman inspector has been appointed to inspect work places where women and children are employed.
[5]Utah, Laws 1913, C. 63.

(3) EDUCATIONAL LAWS

Next in order for consideration are the indirect measures, that is, compulsory educational laws, which are in force in Utah and serve to mitigate child labor.

These enactments in the main go hand in hand with the direct legislative acts already cited; and, it will be noted that they are desirable supplementary, almost indispensable measures in connection with restrictive child labor laws. Prohibitive legislation for children in regard to entrance into industry is not all that is desired in promoting their well-being. The time they may not spend in industry is to be devoted to such training as will more adequately equip them, mentally and physically, for adult life.

Social workers in our country have frequently pointed out that children need leisure time for play and wholesome recreation, but they have also recognized the importance of preventing children from simply drifting along in idleness. Part of their leisure time becomes a valuable asset to them, and in turn to society, when they are given an opportunity to take up some line of work or study which will develop their mental and physical powers as well as enable them to form habits of industry and application.

Quite general approval is given to the view that considerable practical training for boys and girls can be secured through our public school system. Certainly, for children fourteen to eighteen years of age, who must become wage-earners on leaving school, industrial and vocational training will be useful to them, particularly as applied to mechanical and agricultural employment.[1]

The Constitution[2] of the State of Utah made it mandatory upon the legislature to maintain a uniform system of education for all the children of the state. The public school system was to include kindergarten schools, common schools, usually known as grade schools; secondary schools or high schools; an agricultural

---

[1] In this connection, Professor H. R. Seager in an article, entitled, "Program of Social Legislation," states: "Parallel with restrictions on the hours of labor of children and women must go better and better provisions for industrial training. . . . This country affords unrivalled opportunities for the efficient worker, and the elevation of standards of living will depend more than on anything on the sort of equipment for the working life we provide for those who must be self-supporting." American Association for Labor Legislation Publications, 1908-1910, Proceedings of the First Annual Meeting, 1907, p. 102.

[2] Utah, Constitution, Art. 10.

college; a university; and such other schools as the legislature found necessary to establish. In fact it provided for an expansion of the system established in the earlier territorial period.

A broad and comprehensive law was passed by the state legislature in 1897,[1] under the mandatory provisions of the State Constitution relating to education within the commonwealth. This measure carried forward the subject of compulsory school attendance as recorded in the territorial law.[2] Children between eight and fourteen years of age were now required to attend school at least twenty weeks of each year, ten of which must be consecutive. Exceptions were allowed in cases where children were excused for cause by school officials. A reasonable excuse from such duty included cases where the services of children were necessary for the support of their parents, a widowed mother or invalid father.

Parents or guardians of children not complying with the act were guilty of a misdemeanor.

The subsequent sessions of the legislature passed a number of educational bills, but the subject matter in these enactments is not pertinent to our treatise. However, in the measure passed in 1905,[3] the question of school attendance again received attention.

The required period of school attendance, for children eight to sixteen years of age, was placed at twenty weeks, ten of which must be consecutive in each school year. In this connection, also, the law further provided that in cities of the first and second class, the attendance period should be thirty weeks, ten of which must be consecutive in each school year.

It is necessary to pass to a recent period to find other educational measures pertinent to our subject. An act was passed by the legislature in 1919,[4] which provided for part-time schools and made attendance compulsory upon all minors in industry up to eighteen years of age. In brief, the law requires compulsory school attendance for minors under eighteen years of age, for at least thirty weeks of each school year; except for children legally employed who must attend day-time continuation schools at least 144 hours per year.

[1]Utah, Laws 1897, p. 49.
[2]See C. II, p. 36.
[3]Utah, Laws 1905, C. 95.
[4]Utah, Laws 1919, C. 92.

The enforcement of the measure is entrusted to truant officers or special employment attendance officers, and like the earlier school laws, violation of the act is a misdemeanor.

At the same session of the legislature, in 1919, a vocational educational measure was also passed to promote education in agriculture, trades and industries. The State Board of Education administers the law and cooperates with the Federal Government for the promotion of vocational education.

5. ADMINISTRATION OF THE CHILD LABOR LAWS

In the foregoing discussion, authorities responsible for the administration of labor laws have been only briefly referred to; it is necessary, therefore, to comment a little more fully on this phase of the child labor legislation.

In brief, the following authorities are entrusted with the enforcement of the child labor laws: (1) school authorities, who issue certificates of age, schooling, and of literacy for children legally employed; and their agents, truant officers, entrusted with the enforcement of compulsory school laws; (2) the State Board of Health who enforce sanitary laws and those special provisions of the child labor laws that relate to dangerous trades and the general health and morals of minors; (3) Juvenile Court officials to whom cases are brought and who have final jurisdiction where custody or legal punishment of a child is in question; and, (4) the State Industrial Commission administers and enforces all child labor laws.

The effective administration of child labor laws is a matter of importance. The constitutionality of these laws have not given rise to legal controversy, since the minor is considered a ward of the state, but the difficulty arises rather in connection with their enforcement, for it is generally conceded that laws are of little value unless adequately enforced.[1]

---

[1] A number of studies consulted seem to show that the child labor laws of our country in general are very often inadequately enforced. In this connection, the words of Dr. Clopper are significant. He states: "Our compulsory school attendance laws, our child labor laws, our delinquency laws, our dependency laws, our health laws, and all our other laws that seek to train, protect and nurture children are, generally speaking, inadequately administered by truancy, labor, and probation, parole and health officers." (The American Child, Published by the National Child Labor Committee, Nov. 1919, p. 209.) See also Studies in Economic Relations of Women, Vol. 2, Labor Laws and Their Enforcement, Weakness of the Massachusetts Child Labor Laws, by Grace F. Ward.

In Utah, as we have already pointed out, the problem of child labor has not become acute in any way, but sufficient attention no doubt has not been given to the enforcement of child labor legislation. With the creation, however, of a State Industrial Commission and with an increased number of inspectors more attention can now be given to this work. Again, careful attention to the adjustment of penalties to offences is of imporance. Progress, however, ultimately depends upon the constant vigilance of the public. Good child labor laws are enacted and properly enforced only by an awakened and interested public.[1]

The standard set by the child labor laws of Utah approaches the goal desired for child labor legislation. The question, however, of the employment of children in industry has become more than a state affair. It is generally thought that state efforts must be supplemented by Federal action. Something has already been attempted along this line, and probably more will be accomplished in the near future to supplement the child labor enactments of the various states of the Union.[2]*

[1]The enforcement of child labor laws is further treated in Chapter IV, in connection with the enforcement of labor laws affecting the employment of women.

[2]Commons and Andrews are of the opinion that federal legislation is needed for the sake of uniformity in enforcement of child labor laws as well as for uniformity in restrictions on child labor. They say: "For the better enforcement of child labor laws cooperation between all the different agencies that are interested is essential. The standards which have been and will be established in regard to the entrance of children into industry will never be thoroughly enforced until the problem of administration is taken up with the same enthusiasm and persistence which have marked campaigns for legislation." (Commons, John R., and Andrews, J. B., Rev. ed. 1920, p. 346.)

*Congress passed a child labor law in 1916. This measure excluded from interstate commerce goods made in factories where children under fourteen years of age were employed, or where children between fourteen and sixteen years of age worked more than eight hours a day, or six days a week, or did night work. Professor Charles A. Beard states in "American Government and Politics" (3d ed. 1921, p. 386) that, "This measure came before the Supreme Court of the United States in the case of Hammer V. Dagenhart, 247 U. S. 251, in 1918 and was declared unconstitutional by vote of five to four judges. The court held that the child labor law was not really a regulation of interstate commerce, but a regulation of the conditions of manufacturing within the states. It was also contended in the court that the law usurped powers reserved to the states by the Tenth Amendment to the Constitution and would deprive citizens of their property without due process of law as provided in the Fifth Amendment. An attempt was then made to prevent child labor by federal act (Revenue Act of 1918,) through the exercise of taxing power—heavily taxing the profits of companies using child labor—thus indirectly accomplishing the same results."

The federal act based on the taxing power of the government placed a

6. SUMMARY

The legislation affecting the employment of children in Utah has been aimed primarily at keeping them out of industry. By successive steps the minimum age of employment in manufacturing and mercantile pursuits has been raised to sixteen years, unless they are legally permitted to enter these industries. These restrictive measures set a standard as high as that of any state in the Union.

These child labor laws have been supplemented by far reaching educational requirements which aim to insure the attendance of children in the public schools until they are allowed to enter into industry, and when adequately enforced these compulsory school laws constitute an effective method of lessening child labor if not almost making it a negligible factor in industry.

Examination of the child labor laws also brings out the fact that they specify a list of occupations from which children are excluded without employment certificates. In view of the fact, that industrial conditions are constantly changing the list of occupations given can hardly cover, for any length of time, all kinds of employment which endanger the life and health of children. It is true that the laws do give the State Board of Health the right to exclude children from occupations thought to be injurious to them, but possibly an improvement in the laws might result from the use of a general term to cover all kinds of gainful occupations deemed undesirable (rather than a specified list) with the possible exception of agriculture and domestic service. Even here observation leads to the thought that the laws might contain provisions for age requirements and hours of labor.[1]

It seems also, in connection with employment certificates, that a too liberal use of exemptions tends to make child labor laws futile. Care, therefore, should be exercised in this matter, and furthermore, when children are granted employment certificates they are not to be forgotten by school authorities and health

prohibitive tax of 10 per cent on the annual net profits of any enterprises that employed children in violation of the standard named. A case was before the United States Supreme Court in 1920 to test the constitutionality of this measure. (Commons, J. R., and Andrews, J. B., Principles of Labor Legislation, Rev. ed. pp. 335-336.)

[1]Too long hours of work in beet fields and canning factories may be injurious to youthful workers as well as long hours in mills, shops, or factories.

officers. Constant vigilance is desirable to keep check on these children. Physical examinations given periodically and preferably in places where children work, are advisable to safeguard their interest and welfare; night work under all conditions ought to be prohibited.

In view of the fact that the employment of children is generally recognized as undesirable in the public interest too much attention cannot be given to education and training of children before they enter into industry. In this respect, therefore, the steps taken by the State of Utah to furnish all children better educational advantages are commendable. Even from the commercial point of view increased expenditure of public money for vocational training will undoubtedly yield rich returns in the way of higher industrial efficiency of the youth of the state, when allowed to enter into industry.

Well may we argue that the health and welfare of children[1] are factors which go far to determine the vigor of a people. To promote the best interest of the child is to build up and perfect the coming man.

[1] Fittingly has Dr. E. T. Devine pointed out the fundamental elements to recognize in the interest of the child. In an article, entitled, "The New View of the Child," he says: "The fundamental elements for the welfare of the child are, normal birth, physical protection, joyous infancy, useful education, and an ever fuller inheritance of the accumulated riches of civilization." (Supplement, The Annals of the American Academy of Political and Social Science, July, 1918, Vol. 32, p. 10.)

CHAPTER IV

LEGISLATION AFFECTING THE EMPLOYMENT OF WOMEN

1. WOMEN IN INDUSTRY

(1) EXTENT

Until comparatively recent years women in Utah were not employed as wage-earners, but were busied about their household duties. With changing industrial life in the state, however, the tendency has been for women to gradually enter economic life as wage-earners.

The Federal Census of 1910 showed that there were over 18,000 women in the state, sixteen years of age and over, gainfully employed.[1] This approximately represents about 17 per cent of the total female population sixteen years of age and over.

The occupational statistics presented in Chapter I show the various industries women enter, and it is clear that their employment is not so much in connection with general factory work, but rather in mercantile establishments, the teaching profession and domestic service.

(2) CAUSES

The principal causes of the employment of women in gainful occupations are: (1) the economic reason, cases arising where the earnings of women are necessary for the support of the family; (2) where employers substitute women for men in certain kinds of employment because they will accept lower wages, or because of their greater fitness for certain employments; (3) the use of improved machinery in industrial plants which does not require technical skill to handle, likewise serving as an inducement to substitute women for men; (4) a desire on the part of many young women workers, who are not under necessity to work, to have something to do to fill the gap between school days and marriage.

[1]See C. I, pp. 24-28.

(3) THE LABOR OF WOMEN

Most of the legislation for women in Utah has been directed toward the health and safety of female employees: shortening the hours of work for women, eliminating night work as well as increasing wages, and bettering conditions of employment. And as in the case of children, the women's clubs and the labor organizations have led in the movement for the enactment of laws looking to the welfare of women workers.

2. LEGISLATION FOR THE PROTECTION OF WORKING WOMEN

(1) HEALTH AND SAFETY MEASURES

In the preceding chapter mention was made of the Mines and Smelter Act of 1896 wherein the legislature in accordance with a mandatory provision of the Constitution prohibited the employment of women and children in mines and smelters, therefore, we need not speak further of this act.

This measure, however, was amended in 1917,[1] changing the prohibitive age period for children to sixteen years, but otherwise leaving the act, so far as it relates to women, unchanged.

At the second session of the state legislature, held in 1897, a measure[2] was enacted looking further to the health of women and girl employees. Proprietors or managers of stores, hotels, and restaurants were required to provide chairs or other contrivances where their female helpers might rest when not employed in the discharge of their respective duties.

The violation of the act was a misdemeanor, but the real value of the enactment as a health measure depended largely upon the kindly feeling of the employer toward his female employees, rather than in an effort of state officials to enforce it.

(2) HOURS OF EMPLOYMENT

Hours legislation for women workers in Utah has been to fix a daily and weekly limitation of hours in the principal industrial occupations in which women are usually employed.

The movement to limit hours of labor for women workers has been comparatively speaking, a recent one in this state. A law limiting hours of employment for female workers was enacted in

[1]Utah, Laws 1917, C. 80.
[2]Utah, Laws 1897, C. 11.

1911.[1] This measure established the nine-hour day and the fifty-four hour week for women. The act was made to cover a wide range of industrial occupations where women work. The list of occupations included mechanical and mercantile establishments as well as laundries, hotels, restaurants, hospitals and telephone and express companies. Domestic service and farm labor, however, were not included in the measure.

The exemption provision of the act related to cases of emergency in hospitals and to such cases where materials were liable to spoil by the enforcement of the law.

The penalty for the violation of the act was a fine—"not less than twenty-five dollars nor more than one hundred dollars, and costs of prosecution."

The State Bureau of Labor, established in 1911, was entrusted with the enforcement of the act.[2] This bureau was under the control of a commissioner who was given power to appoint a deputy commissioner to assist him in the discharge of his official duties.

Section 4 (of Chapter 113, Laws of Utah, 1911), gives the duties of the commissioner as follows: "It shall be the duty of the commissioner to investigate and report to the proper authorities, all violations of the law regarding the conditions surrounding the employment of children, minors and women and the laws established for the protection of all employees in factories, mines, mills and other institutions where labor is employed and to make such recommendation in relation thereto as he may deem proper for the protection of employees. In case any owner or occupant or his agent, shall refuse to admit any officer of said bureau to his workshop or factory, mine or smelter, store or hotel, when open, or in operation, or shall wilfully give false information concerning the same, he shall be guilty of a misdemeanor for each and every offense, and upon conviction thereof shall be subject to a fine of not more than $50 or less than $10 or by imprisonment not to exceed fifteen days."

[1] Utah, Laws 1911, C. 133.
[2] Chapter 113, Laws of Utah, 1911, established the Bureau of Immigration, Labor and Statistics. Prior to this time the state had established a Bureau of Statistics to secure statistical data concerning mining, manufacturing, and farming within the commonwealth.

The law undoubtedly was ambiguous in reference to the term "emergency". Various interpretations might be given to this word which would have a tendency to lessen the value of the act as a protective measure for women wage-earners. This defect was recognized by the Bureau of Labor. Never-the-less on the whole, it worked fairly well. While violations were frequent at first, in a short time, the act appeared to gain in favor among employers, who without much inconvenience adjusted their business to meet its requirements.

Some four years later, 1915, a law[1] was placed upon the statute books regulating the closing hours of mercantile establishments in cities of 10,000 population and over. This included Salt Lake and Ogden where the greatest number of women were gainfully employed.

"Except for the period of six business days immediately preceding December 25, of each year," the business concerns in the above mentioned cities were to close at six o'clock in the evening. Exemptions, however, were made for drug stores and business houses dealing mainly in provisions of a perishable nature; foodstuffs, meats, etc., regarded as public necessities.

Very little was accomplished by this measure to regulate the hours of labor for women. The constitutionality of the law was soon challenged in the courts by individuals charged by the Labor Bureau as violators of the act. The Supreme Court declared the law to be class legislation, and invalid as an exercise of the police power.[2]*

In 1919,[3] the nine-hour law for women, already referred to as the law of 1911, was amended to provide for an eight-hour day and a forty-eight hour week for women workers; and further, the working period of eight hours was to be worked within two periods and within twelve consecutive hours.

The exemptions provided for in the act related to cases of emergency where life and property were in imminent danger, and in packing and canning industries handling perishable fruits and vegetables. In these special industries, women were allowed to work over time in the rush season.

Penalty for the violation of the enactment was the same as provided in the law of 1911, that is, a fine ranging from $25 to

[1]Utah, Laws of 1915, C. 23.
[2]Saville v. Corless 46 U. 495. (1915).
*See page 64 for an account of the case before the Supreme Court of Utah.
[3]Utah, Laws 1919, 70.

$100. The State Federation of Labor and the State Industrial Commission, established in 1917, favored the enactment of the bill.[1] The measure was regarded as a forward step in the interest of female workers.[2]

(3) MINIMUM WAGE SCALE FOR WOMEN

In many respects, of all recent legislation in this country affecting women workers, the laws which established minimum wage rates are among the most important. The question of wages is always one of practical importance in connection with the life and health of workers. Commons and Andrews regard minimum wage laws as, "marking a new stage in the long line of attempts to equalize the power of employer and employee in making the wage bargain."[3] Massachusetts has the distinction of being the first American state to pass a minimum wage law. This commonwealth enacted such a measure in 1912. One year later, however, eight other states had passed minimum wage laws, and among this number was the state of Utah. The Federation of Women's Clubs was the first to propose such legislation in Utah and largely as a result of their efforts a minimum wage law was passed in 1913.[4]

No commission was appointed to make an investigation of wages paid to women, but legislative hearings were held and club women, merchants, manufacturers and employees were called on for testimony. A bill was drafted which seemed to meet the approval of the parties consulted. The women members of the legislature and the Women's Clubs, however, regarded the measure as a compromise bill rather than one which provided adequate wage protection for women workers.

The Utah statute fixed the legal minimum rate for women gainfully employed as follows: For females under eighteen years not less than 75 cents a day; over eighteen, learners and appren-

---

[1]See Proceedings of the 15th Convention of Utah State Federation of Labor, 1919, p. 16. See also the Report of the Industrial Commission of Utah, 1917-1918, p. 12.

[2]In recent years, the movement limiting hours of labor for women has been quite general in the United States. At the beginning of last year, (1920), however, only two states, California and Utah, and the District of Columbia and Porto Rico, had established an eight-hour day and a forty-eight hour week. (Commons, J. R., and Andrews, J. B., Principles of Labor Legislation, Rev. ed. 1920, p. 237.

[3]Commons, J. R., and Andrews, J. B., Principles of Labor Legislation, Rev. ed. 1920, p. 182.

[4]Utah, Laws 1913, C. 63.

tices for the first year, 90 cents a day; and experienced adult workers, $1.25 a day.

The enforcing authority was placed with the Commissioner of Labor and later with the State Industrial Commission,[1] when this Commission assumed the duties of the Labor Department.

(a) WEAKNESS OF THE MINIMUM WAGE LAW

While the scope of the application of minimum wage laws may vary, the general purpose of such legislation is to prohibit the employment of women and minors at excessively low wages. Certainly, also, wage investigations made at different times in a number of states, affirm the fact that many women receive wages that are not sufficient to supply them with the ordinary comforts of life.

The minimum wage law of Utah has in a number of cases slightly increased the wages of young women, but on the whole little can be said in favor of the law as it now stands. The rates fixed are too low to give much protection to women wage-earners. According to the report of the Commissioner of Labor: "The Utah female wage scale provides for a smaller wage than that fixed by any wage scale commission in any other state."[2*]

At best possibly the greatest good the law has done has been in calling the attention of employers and employees, and the public to some of the inconsistences and discrepancies which exist in the wage system.

The defects of the law are that it sets a low standard and is inflexible. While employers in the main pay a higher wage than the law calls for there is a tendency on the part of others to make the minimum wage the maximum wage. Again, a law fixing wage rates seven years ago cannot be a fair standard under the conditions now existing.

In this connection, a brief extract from the report of the State

---

[1]See Chapter VI for an account of the duties and powers of the Industrial Commission.

[2]Utah Facts and Figures, 1913-1914, p. 13.

*Professor Thomas Harrison Reed writes: "The method of fixing a minimum wage by legislative enactment must necessarily be arbitrary. What may be a satisfactory minimum wage in one year, under a given condition with regard to prices will be entirely insufficient or excessively high the next. The alternative is to intrust the task to an administrative commission." Reed, T. H., Form and Functions of American Government, p. 440.

Industrial Commission may be offered. The report reads: "The minimum wage law should be amended . . . . . . The wage established by law was inadequate from the beginning. Since the increased cost of living, it is pitifully low and works a great hardship on the girls and women who are forced to accept it."[1]

A bill to amend the minimum wage law was introduced into the legislature in 1919, and while the measure passed the House, it was defeated in the Senate.

A "flat rate" law, such as the law of Utah, prescribing a legal minimum wage is rare. Only one other State, Arizona, has a fixed state wide flat rate law.[2] The Arkansas Law,[3] however, modifies this system of fixing a flat rate daily wage, in that a commission has power to either raise or lower the wage rate. The vast majority of minimum wage laws in this country provide for wage boards or commissions with authority, after careful investigation, to fix different wage rates in various industries and localities.

A regular so called, "flat rate" law, of the Utah type, tends to prevent this careful adjustment of rates for various industries and localities. Again, a law of uniform rates makes revisions difficult in periods of rapidly changing prices such as we have just experienced during the last three or four years. Furthermore, it is doubtful if a "flat rate" law calls forth the active interest of employers and employees in like degree where wages are regulated by commissions. Most students of this problem favor the commission type as being more advantageous to the welfare of women workers.[4]

[1] Report of the Industrial Commission of Utah, 1917-1918, p. 12.
[2] Arizona, Laws 1917, C. 38.
[3] Arkansas, Laws 1915, No. 291.
[4] In a recent report of the State Industrial Commission, the inspector for women writes: "The minimum wage fixed by state law is too small to warrant very many violations. During the war, the minimum was lost sight of because of the scarcity of help. Women were paid the wages they demanded and needed because of the increased cost of living. However, since the war ended, some employers are now keeping strictly to the minimum which makes it very hard, indeed, for the girls and women compelled to work for such a small pittance in view of the fact that living conditions are still high.

"There is but one just law, and that is for the legislature to do as other states have done, to give to the Industrial Commission the power to establish wage boards, under such a system employers and employees alike will receive just consideration." Report of the Industrial Commission of Utah, July 1, 1918 to June 30, 1920, p. 191.

(4) SOCIAL INSURANCE

The question of social insurance, that is, insurance which provides for state action in alleviating distress which falls upon wage-earners or persons similarly situated, as a result of accident, sickness, and premature death of the chief wage-earner of the family, has developed in Utah principally in connection with workmen's insurance and benefit funds; and of this we shall speak in a subsequent chapter.

The social insurance discussed here is that of mothers' aid or insurance for widows with dependent children.

The law to aid dependent mothers in Utah is similar to the mothers' aid laws which have been so generally accepted throughout our country. The principle underlying the plan seems to be an outgrowth of outdoor relief with a desire to prevent more and more the need for public and private charity. Again, child helping agencies have advocated keeping the family together as far as possible. The straight pension, or pecuniary benefits allowed is based upon condition that mothers are capable of providing a proper home for their children.

Missouri and Illinois were the first states of the Union to pass mothers' aid laws—enacting such measures in 1911[1]. Two years later, Utah had passed a measure providing for the partial support of dependent mothers.

The Utah Act of 1913[2] authorized county commissioners, in counties with a population less than 125,000 people to raise a fund not to exceed $10,000 in any one year for the support of mothers dependent upon their own efforts for the maintenance of their children. In counties with a population of 125,000 or more the authority devolved upon the Judge of the Juvenile Court.

The law further provided that an allowance of $10 per month be granted to a dependent mother having one child under fifteen years of age, and $5 for each of the other children under this age.

Since this law was enacted it has been amended several times. In 1915,[3] the legislature raised the amount of the fund to $20,000 in counties with a population of 100,000 or more. Again, in 1919,[4] another amendment was made in the law making the following changes: (1) County Commissioners in their respective jurisdictions were given complete jurisdiction in regard to this

[1]See Warner, Amos, American Charities, Rev. ed. p. 356.
[2]Utah, Laws 1913, C. 90.
[3]Utah, Laws 1915, C. 21.
[4]Utah, Laws 1919, C. 77.

act; (2) no specific allowance for each child was mentioned in the measure, but a more general clause was included to the effect that the allowance to any dependent mother should not exceed $40 a month whether she had one or more children under sixteen years of age; and further the amount was to be determined by the County Commissioners; (3) persons receiving the benefits of this act were required to reside in the county where aid was given for a period of two years before making application for allowance.

The law has had a beneficial effect by alleviating distress in such cases as, premature death of the chief wage-earner of a family, where a widowed mother is left in rather poor circumstances. On the other hand, County Commissioners do not always give due consideration to applications for allowance, and where this occurs, the law does not always reach the most worthy cases. As time goes on, however, possibly more attention will be given to the question of adopting a standardized system more in harmony with other forms of social insurance which are gradually gaining ground in the state.

3. ADMINISTRATION

The question of administration is of importance in connection with the discussion of legislation looking to the welfare of women workers. Possibly, the most difficult problem in this respect centers about the enforcement of hours legislation. Violation of hour limitation for women is more difficult to discover than violations which refer to safety and sanitary regulations. Often a single inspection will reveal a violation of a safety or sanitary measure, while regulation of hours of work refers to a continuing condition which is obviously more difficult to detect.

The Department of Labor appointed deputies to look after matters pertaining to hour laws for females as well as the minimum wage law. In 1911-1912 just after the establishing by law of a nine-hour day for women the Department of Labor investigated over 150 cases of alleged violations of this measure. In the majority of these cases the parties complained against were guilty, but the department was often unable to secure evidence which county attorneys required to bring the cases before the courts. Females required to work in excess of required hours refused to appear against the offending proprietors for fear of losing their positions.[1]

[1]See Report of the State Bureau of Immigration, Labor and Statistics, 1911-1912, pp. 28-29.

While investigations were made in a number of cases due to complaints of women workers themselves, by far the majority of cases came to the attention of the Labor Department by persons not directly interested or through relatives and friends of the workers.

The policy of the enforcing authority in the investigation of alleged violations of this first hour limitation law was one of leniency. Before formal legal complaints were made against offending parties they were given an opportunity to regulate their hours of labor for female employees to conform to the law.

While fairly enforcing the nine-hour law for women, the Labor Department recognized the fact that to thoroughly enforce the measure would require more inspectors than were employed for this purpose.[1]

(1) THE ENFORCEMENT OF THE EIGHT HOUR LAW

For the period from July 1, 1918 to June 30, 1920, the State Industrial Commission reports that there were 765 inspections of places where women and children were gainfully employed. These inspections included department stores, factories and canneries; and in fact, all places within the state where women and children were employed, except in domestic service and agriculture including beet fields, orchards and farms.

The report gives 94 violations of the eight-hour day and four violations of the minimum wage law.

The Labor Inspector points out that a number of the violations related to instances where girls desired to obtain extra money by working overtime.

On the whole the report shows that notwithstanding the number of violations that the eight-hour law is very generally observed by employers everywhere in the state, and that there is little disposition on the part of employers to take advantage of the emergency clause of the law.[2]

In the enforcement of the minimum wage law, the Labor Department adopted the following plan. Prior to the time the law became effective blanks were sent to all employers of female workers in the state to secure information as to the number of their employees, with classification for minors, learners and

See Report of the State Bureau of Immigration, Labor and Statistics, 1911-1912, pp. 28-29.

[2]See Report of the Industrial Commission of Utah, Period, July 1, 1918 to June 30, 1920, pp. 190-191.

experienced women workers. At the same time, information was obtained as to the amount of wages paid employees as above classified. This information was carefully checked and notification given to cases where the pay rolls did not conform to the new law.

When the law became effective, representatives of the department visited practically every city and town in the state to see that the act was observed. In many instances visits were made at various intervals to stores, factories, and work shops. Pay rolls of a number of establishments, where women were employed, were examined when doubt was entertained in regard to the observance of the measure.[1]

During the first twenty months of the operation of the law several hundred violations of the act had been investigated. Only six cases, however, were brought before the courts. Practically all violations were settled without prosecution by employers paying their female help the deficiencies in wages due them. In this manner, for the period referred to above, some $8,000 were collected in back wages.

According to an earlier report issued by the State Industrial Commission covering a period of one year, July 1, 1917 to June 30, 1918, some six hundred inspections were made of stores, factories, laundries, and other places where women were employed. These investigations resulted in the detection of fifty violations of the "nine-hour law" and but from this number only two arrests were made, and one conviction resulted. There were ten violations of the minimum wage law, but in each case the amount due employees was collected and paid to them.[2]

The vast majority of the employers showed a willingness to cooperate with the Industrial Commission in carrying out the labor laws.[3] This assistance has undoubtedly greatly facilitated the inspection of conditions concerning employees. It is rare now to find an instance where the minimum wage is not paid.

4. CONSTITUTIONALITY

There has been some litigation arising from the constitution-

[1] When the State Bureau of Immigration, Labor and Statistics was established in 1911 (Laws of Utah, 1911, C. 113), the commissioner of labor was authorized to inspect stores, factories, and work shops where minors and women were employed. In 1917 the State Industrial Commission became the Commissioner of Immigration, Labor and Statistics and this Commission enjoyed similar powers. An account is given in Chapter VI of the duties and powers of the Industrial Commisson.

[2] Report of the State Industrial Commission, 1917-1918, p. 11.

[3] See Report of the State Industrial Commission, 1917-1918, p. 12.

ality of laws relating to women workers. The hour law for women has been very generally recognized as protective legislation coming within the police power of the State. On the other hand, a number of employers were inclined to consider the minimum wage law when enacted as beyond constitutional limits. The Supreme Court of Oregon, however, upheld the constitutionality of the minimum wage law of that state[1] and the same case was affirmed in a recent decision of the Supreme Court of the United States.[2]

One friendly case was brought before the Supreme Court of Utah to test the constitutionality of the minimum wage law, and the court postponed the case to ascertain the result of the Oregon case. In view of the decision of the Oregon Court which in turn was affirmed by the Supreme Court of the United States the case was never argued in the Utah court.

It seems fairly safe to say that the general idea which prevails among the people is that the awarding of a living wage to workers is not an unreasonable or an arbitrary power in violation of the public policy of the State.

A second case[3] which came before the State Supreme Court was relative to the closing hours of mercantile establishments in cities of ten thousand population and over. Chapter 23, Laws of Utah, 1915, required: "That all mercantile and commercial houses either wholesale or retail, or both, in cities of ten thousand population and over, shall close at six o'clock in the evening of every day of the year, except for the period of six business days immediately preceding December 25, of each year."

Walter Saville, a merchant selling men's clothing, boots, shoes, etc., in Salt Lake City, and William Porizky, engaged in selling cigars at retail in Salt Lake City, sold goods after 6 p. m.

The plaintiffs, held in custody by John S. Corless, Sheriff of Salt Lake County, asked to be discharged on the ground, "that the act contravenes the Fourteenth Amendment to the Constitution of the United States, and the State Constitution, forbidding special legislation where a general law can be made applicable."

The act was defended on the ground that it was a police measure.

The Court held the act unconstitutional on the ground: (1) "The business conducted by the plaintiffs does not affect the

[1]Stettler v. O'Hara, 69 Ore. 519, (1914).

[2]Stettler v. O'Hara, 243 U. S., 629, 37 Sup. Ct. 475, (1917).

[3]Saville v. Corless, Sheriff and Porizky v. Same, 46 U. 495, (1915), 151 Pac. 51.

health or safety of those engaged in it. **Nor is the act directed
to enterprises affecting health, morals, safety, or general welfare . . . . It, therefore, cannot be upheld as**
a police measure"; (2) The act was special legislation; "It only
applies to cities of 10,000 population and over . . . .
The act further exempts drug stores, and commercial houses
dealing in . . . . foodstuffs and provisions of a perishable nature"; (3) The act violated the constitutional right,
"to enjoy, acquire and possess property the most valuable of
which is . . . . . that of the right to vend and sell."

The law for the support of widowed mothers has likewise
been brought before the Supreme Court of Utah to test the constitutionality of the act. The court held, that the law "defined
and declared a policy of the state," within the province of the
legislature . . . . . "having in mind the public welfare by
assisting in surrounding children of tender age home association
and with the care and nurture of their natural protector, the
mother."[1]

5. SUMMARY OF PRESENT SITUATION AND
TENDENCIES

We may reasonably say that some progress has been made
in Utah in the safeguarding of women in industry.

It is to be hoped, however, that the legislation of the past
may serve as a foundation and encouragement for better legislation in the near future, because the standards in Utah have
lagged behind those in so many sister states.

A substantial beginning has been made through legislation
in regulating wages, hours of labor, and working conditions for
women. Much more, however, remains to be done.

Questions of importance which call for further consideration
may be grouped under four or five heads.

(1) The adjustment of hours to the special dangers of specific industries. Studies which have been made in various
countries show that certain occupations which women enter are
not only more dangerous than others, but also more fatiguing.[2]

A few states of our Union are approaching this view. Kansas,
Oregon, and Washington have commissions to determine maxi-

---

[1]D. & R. G. R. R. v. Grand County, 51 U. 294, (1914).

[2]Investigations have been made in England in the match industry and
in Canada in the employment of telephone operators. (See King, W. L.
Mackenzie, Industry and Humanity, pp. 317-330.)

mum periods for different industries. The idea being that a woman is not to be employed for any period of time "dangerous to her health, safety, and welfare."[1]

Commons and Andrews in "Principles of Labor Legislation," consider this matter of significance. They tell us that precaution taken to preserve a statutory limit of hours through administrative rulings "marks a decided advance toward accomplishing the real purpose of hour limitations, the prevention of fatigue by forbidding excessive hours of work."[2]

It seems reasonable to conclude that adjusting hours according to the strain of specific occupations as a means of safeguarding the worker's health is superior to the ordinary law making a general limit for all industries.

(2) The desirability of fixing minimum wage standards which allow workers a "minimum comfort level". Progress toward this goal may possibly come from investigations of wage boards or industrial commissions. Such a safeguard will be beneficial to the health and welfare of workers, and in turn beneficial to society in general.

(3) Too little attention has been given to the question of rest periods, overtime work, and the health of workers in general.

(4) Greater attention to the question of social insurance. Commons and Andrews have pointed out that, "If insurance is to accomplish its object of conserving the health and life of a nation, it is desirable that maternity benefits be extended as widely as possible."[3]

[1]Commons, J. R., and Andrews, J. B., Principles of Labor Legislation, Rev. ed. p. 280.
[2]Commons, J. R., and Andrews, J. B., Principles of Labor Legislation, Rev. ed. p. 241.
[3]Ibid., p. 425.

CHAPTER V

LEGISLATION AFFECTING ADULT MALE WORKERS

Since workingmen form the great bulk of the wage-earners of the state, we may expect our discussion in this chapter to be somewhat extended as compared with our examination of the labor laws for women and children.

1. EXTENT

The occupation statistics presented in Chapter I show that there were in Utah in 1910, 123,112 males sixteen years of age and over. Of this number, a little over 89 per cent, or 110,302, were gainfully employed. In 1920 there were 127,417 males (10 years of age and over) gainfully employed.[1]

2. WAGES

In Chapter II of this study, attention was given to the steps taken in the territorial period of Utah's history to protect the wages of workmen. Following up the earlier account, we shall find that the laws passed since statehood, dealing with this subject, extend the safeguard to laborers and mechanics generally in regard to claims for wages.

(1) LIEN LAWS—WAGE PREFERENCE

In 1896,[2] the Law of 1892[3] was repealed and a new measure enacted. This act provided that in cases of assignment or receivership of property due to the suspension of business by action of creditors, wages due laborers, or servants for labor performed within one year just prior to the seizure or transfer of such property should be treated as preferred debt and such employees or servants were to be preferred creditors. The law also stipulated the manner of filing claims. The claimant under oath was to state the amount of wages due him, the kind of work performed and the time the work was done. In cases where there were insufficient funds to pay these preferred claims in full they were to be paid pro rata after paying all costs occasioned by the seizure of such property.

[1]See C. I, pp. 24-28.
[2]Utah, Laws 1896, C. 49.
[3]See C. II, p. 35.

This law was supplemented by another measure[1] passed at the same session of the legislature. This act required laborers and mechanics to file their accounts at least fifteen days before suit was brought that due notice might be given to the defendant. The measure further provided that a plaintiff be allowed a reasonable attorney's feet in addition to the amount due and owing for wages, but not to exceed $25. This latter provision, no doubt, made it somewhat easier for employees, servants, and laborers to obtain the protection of the law.

About a decade later; that is, in 1905,[2] the legislature enacted a measure to hold municipalities jointly liable with contractors for wages or money owing to persons furnishing labor and material for public works.

Some time elapsed before any further steps were taken by the legislature in respect to wages as a preferred claim or debt. In 1913, several amendments were made to the earlier laws dealing with this subject.

The first amendment[3] stipulated the amount which might be assigned by statutory or trusteeship agreements to preferred creditors. This sum was not to exceed $400 for any one claimant. The second amendment[4] in addition to stipulating the maximum amount for any one preferred claimant, sought to regulate the time for which preferred claims were to run. The work performed was to be within five months next preceding the time when the property of any person, firm, or corporation was put into the hands of receivers.

At the regular session of the legislature, in 1917, a further amendment[5] was made to the act of 1905 relating to labor on public works. Not only were contractors required to give bonds for the faithful performance of their contracts on public works, but the enactment made additional provision stipulating that contractors should promptly make payments to all workers supplying labor or furnishing material in the prosecution of the work. The purpose of the measure was to safeguard the wages of employees of contractors.

Similar laws to those just described exist in a score or more of states of the Union, and courts have generally given a very liberal construction of these lien laws, in view of their purpose

[1]Utah, Laws 1896, C. 40.
[2]Utah, Laws 1905, C. 87.
[3]Utah, Laws 1913, C. 23.
[4]Utah, Laws 1913, C. 24.
[5]Utah, Laws 1917, C. 36.

to require payment from those who profit by the labor and material furnished by others.[1]

(2) WAGE PAYMENTS

Under the caption of wage payments come two important factors in labor legislation, viz., medium of payment and time of payment.

a. MEDIUM OF PAYMENT

Legislation in our country treats the question of wage payments in connection with company stores and boarding houses, and the legislation seems to fall under three general heads: (1) laws which would eliminate the entire system of company stores; (2) laws which attempt to regulate prices in company stores; (3) laws which permit the system, but which seek to eliminate intimidation or coercion of employees to make use of these institutions. The Utah law on this subject falls under the third class, which is mainly true of agrarian states.

In 1901,[2] a law was enacted in Utah to the effect that no employee must be coerced to trade at any particular store or board at any particular house. Any person seeking to intimidate, threaten or use any undue influence to compel an employee to trade with any store or board at any boarding house was deemed guilty of a misdemeanor.

This is as far as the statutory provision has gone to regulate the medium of wage payments. Yet, we must not overlook the fact that the medium of payment for labor performed has much to do with the freedom of the wage-earner. His liberty depends pretty much on his freedom to buy what and where he wants; furthermore, this freedom is the best safeguard against unwarranted deductions in the worker's earnings.

b. TIME OF PAYMENT

Only recently has a law been passed in Utah concerning the question of wage settlements. In 1919,[3] a measure was enacted requiring a semi-monthly payment of wages in lawful money of the United States or in negotiable checks and drafts convertible into money on demand at their face value, except in cases where

[1]See Clark, L. D., The Law of the Employment of Labor, pp. 60-62, and Paterson, R. G., Wage-Payment Legislation in the United States, Bulletin of the United States Bureau of Labor Statistics, No. 229, 1917.
[2]Utah, Laws 1901, C. 44.
[3]Utah, Laws 1919, C. 71.

agreement existed between an employer and employee for different terms of payment.

The act further made it incumbent upon employers to pay any employee immediately upon discharge. For delay the laborer was entitled to the same rate of wages until paid, provided that in no case was the wages to continue for more than ten days. On the other hand, when the laborer or employee resigned, or quit his employment, the compensation due him was payable at his next regular pay day.

The administration of the law was entrusted to the State Industrial Commission, and violation of the act was made a misdemeanor.

This question of the time and mode of wage payment is always a matter of concern to the laborer. With cash payments the worker can buy where he wants, and with wage payments at frequent intervals he is better able to meet his obligations without extended credit.

The general principles of the act regulating wage payments were proposed in the reports of state officials sometime before action was taken by the legislature. The Commissioner of Labor in his report for the years 1911-1912[1] advocated a law which would require business concerns to settle immediately with employees whom they discharge or who quit their employment. He stated in his report that frequent complaints had been lodged with his office relative to this question of collecting wages upon the severance of employment.

In his next report, two years later, 1913-1914,[2] the Commissioner of Labor again pointed out that his department had received frequent requests to intercede in the collection of wage accounts, therefore, he recommended that the legislature consider the matter and provide an adequate measure for wage settlements.

He further explained that where men depended entirely upon their weekly wages that they needed protection of this kind. He was also of the opinion that there would be fewer petty and major cases of crime if employers were required to make immediate settlement with employees quitting their service. He makes this deduction from the fact that frequently a floating

[1]Report of the Utah State Bureau of Immigration, Labor ahd Statistics, 1911-1912, p. 33.
[2]Report of the Utah State Bureau of Immigration, Labor and Statistics, 1913-1914, p. 16.

population desiring to leave cities and towns are detained in idleness waiting for several days to obtain their wages for services performed; and during this time they are in immediate need of their money for maintenance.

The State Industrial Commission, in 1917, likewise recommended legislation for the collection of wages for labor performed.[1]

It was largely through the persistent request of these officials coming in contact with the question of wage payments that the legislature enacted the measure we have described.

3. HOURS OF LABOR

Hours legislation for workmen in Utah is somewhat fragmentary when compared with the progress made in the regulation of the hours of labor for women and children. Public opinion has hardly yet awakened to the need of legislative action to restrict men's hours of labor in general employment. In the principal cities, however, and in the mining camps hours of labor for men are quite uniform, and the eight-hour day is rather generally observed in employing establishments.

(1) PUBLIC WORKS

The statutory legislation regulating working hours of men is confined to hours of labor on public works and in the hazardous occupations of mining and smelting.

In Chapter II, our attention was called to the Act of 1894 establishing an eight-hour day on public works as applied to the territory of Utah, and to all political subdivisions thereof.

This same principle was also embodied in the State Constitution of 1896. The provision reads as follows: "Eight hours shall constitute a day's work on all works or undertakings carried on or aided by the state, county, or municipal governments."[2]

This prescribed regulation of hours as provided in the Constitution, and as was later applied by statute embodied in the revised statutes of the state for 1898 was amended by the act of 1901.[3] In fixing eight hours as a day's work on all public works, the law was made to apply to both direct and contract work; and further, the measure extended its provisions to impose a penalty

---

[1]Report of the Industrial Commission of Utah, 1917-1918, p. 13.
[2]Utah, State Constitution, Art. 16, Sec. 6.
[3]Utah, Laws 1901, C. 41.

for violation by any public official or contractor. Violation of the
act was made a misdemeanor.

Exceptions for overtime were allowed in cases of emergency,
defined as "imminent danger to life and property."

At the next session of the legislature which met in 1903, a
further amendment was made to the revised statutes of 1898 relating to the eight-hour day on public works. This act[1] reiterated
the provisions of the earlier measure of 1901, but also prescribed
the eight-hour work day for penal institutions in the state.

(2) PRIVATE EMPLOYMENT

a. MINES AND SMELTERS

As pointed out in the introductory chapter the mining industry
has always occupied an important position in the industrial life of
Utah.

Cognizant of the special dangers of mining, the legislature in
the territorial period enacted laws looking to the health and safety
of workers in mines. The state constitution also authorized the
legislature to pass laws looking to the "health and safety of employees in factories, smelters, and mines."[2]

This mandatory clause was complied with in part by the Act
of 1896, and subsequent laws which will be examined in connection with health and safety measures for workmen.

The law of 1896[3] limited the hours to eight in one day as applied to employment in underground mines or working in smelters, and in places for the refining of ores or metals. Exceptions
were allowed for cases of emergency "where life and property
were in imminent danger," which weakened the measure but it
undoubtedly has been helpful in fixing a short working day in
this hazardous industry fraught with danger to the life and
health of many workers.

(3) CONSTITUTIONALITY

So far as we know, hours legislation as applied to public works
has not been questioned in the courts of Utah, and we under-
stand that legislation of this nature has been quite generally

[1]Utah, Laws 1903, C. 98.
[2]Utah, State Constitution, Art. 16, Sec. 6.
[3]Utah, Laws 1896, C. 72.

upheld by the courts of this country.[1] Opposition, however, has been met in attempting to apply the eight-hour day to private employment.

The significant case of Holden v. Hardy[2] arose over the Utah Act of 1896 fixing the eight-hour day for men employed in mines and smelters. This precipitated the greatest controversy that has risen in the state in connection with the constitutionality of any labor law.

The case was of such importance as bearing upon the jurisdiction of the legislature to limit hours of labor for adult workmen in private employment, that Commons and Andrews have been pleased to call this case as marking, "the headlight of a new period,"[3] especially in showing the inequality of the bargaining power of employer and employee. Since the constitutionality of the law was upheld by the State Supreme Court and later by the Supreme Court of the United States, the right to limit working hours of laborers in mines by legislation has practically been undisputed in this country.

Special attention will be given at this point to the instance giving rise to this case as well as pointing out pertinent paragraphs in the decisions of the courts.

The plaintiff, Albert F. Holden, had been convicted by a Justice of the Peace of a misdemeanor for violation of the eight-hour law for working men in underground mines. A fine of $50 was assessed against him, and upon his refusal to pay the same the sheriff, Harvey Hardy, had committed him. To obtain his liberty, he presented a petition for a writ of habeas corpus, contending that the State law, fixing an eight hour day for laborers in mines was unconstitutional in violation of both the Constitution of the United States and the Constitution of the State of Utah.

The plaintiff also contended that the law was class legislation since "it deprived employers and employees in the mining and smelting business of the right to make contracts on the same basis as enjoyed by persons and corporations in other lines of business."

The Supreme Court of the State in reviewing the case cited the provisions of the State Constitution relative to the powers

[1]Clark, L. D., The Law of the Employment of Labor, pp. 73-82.
[2]State v. Holden, 14. U. 71., affirmed, 169, U. S. 366.
[3]Commons, J. R., and Andrews, J. B., Principles of Labor Legislation, Rev. ed. 28.

and duties of the legislature. The Constitution making it mandatory upon the legislature, "that the rights of labor shall have just protection through laws calculated to promote the industrial welfare of the State."[1]

It was also pointed out that the legislature had a constitutional mandate to pass laws, "for the health and safety of employees in factories, smelters and mines."[2]

The Utah Supreme court held that the act was within the police power of the State, and said in part:[3]

"The effort necessary to successful mining, if performed upon the surface of the earth, in pure air and sunlight, prolonged beyond eight-hours, might not be injurious, nor affect the health of able-bodied men. When so extended beneath the surface, in atmosphere laden with gas, and sometimes with smoke, away from the sunlight, it might injuriously affect the health of such persons. It is necessary to use artificial means to supply pure air to men laboring in any considerable distance from the surface. That being so, it is reasonable to assume that the air introduced, when mixed with the impure air beneath the surface, is not as healthful as the breathing of pure air upon the surface. The fact must be conceded that the breathing of pure air is wholesome, and the breathing of impure air is unwholesome. We cannot say that this law, limiting the period of labor to underground mines to eight hours each day, is not calculated to promote health; that it is not adapted to the protection of the health of the class of men who work in underground mines.

"If underground mining is attended with dangers peculiar to it, laws adapted to the protection of such miners from such danger should be confined to that class of mining, and should not include other employments not subject to them. And if men engaged in underground mining are liable to be injured in their health, or otherwise by too long hours labor each day, a law to protect them should be aimed at that peculiar wrong. In this way, laws are enacted to protect people from perils from the operation of railroads, by requiring bells to be rung and whistles sounded at road crossings, and the slacking of the speed of the trains in cities. . . . . . . In this way various classes of business are regulated, and the people protected, by appropriate laws, from dangers and evils that beset them; safety is secured,

[1]Utah, State Constitution, Art. 16. Sec. 1.
[2]Utah, State Constitution, Art. 16, Sec. 1.
[3]Utah v. Holden. 14 U. 71.

health preserved and the happiness and welfare of humanity promoted . . . . The purpose of such laws is not advantage to any person or class of persons, or disadvantage to any person or class of persons. Necessary and just protection is the sole object."

A second case analogous to the one referred to above arose over the employment of a laborer by Albert F. Holden[1] to work in a concentrating mill for the reduction of ores for more than eight hours per day. The State Supreme Court upheld the law on similar grounds to those stated in the case of Utah v. Holden.

In referring to the conditions in concentrating mills and smelters the court said: "Poisonous gases, dust and impalpable substances arise and float in the air in stamp mills, smelters and other works in which ores containing metals, combined with arsenic or other poisonous elements or agencies are treated, reduced, and refined; and there can be no doubt that prolonged effort day after day, subject to such conditions and agencies, will produce morbid, noxious, and often deadly effects in the human system. Some organisms and systems will resist and endure conditions and effects longer than others. It may be said that labor in such conditions must be performed. Granting this, the period of labor each day should be of a reasonable length. Twelve hours per day would be less injurious than fourteen, ten than twelve, and eight than ten. The legislature has named eight. Such a period was deemed reasonable."

In a decision given in 1898, the United States Supreme Court upheld the Utah Eight-Hour Law as a valid exercise of the police power of the State.[2]

In upholding the validity of this state legislation as not in violation of the Fourteenth Amendment to the Federal Constitution, the court said: "This court has not failed to recognize the fact that the law is, to a certain extent, a progressive science; that in some of the states methods of procedure which, at the time the constitution was adopted, were deemed essential to the protection and safety of the people, or to the liberty of the citizen, have been found to be no longer necessary; that restrictions which had formerly been laid upon the conduct of individuals, or of classes of individuals, had proved detrimental

[1]Utah v. Holden, 14 U. 96.
[2]Holden v. Hardy, 169 U. S. 366, 18 Sup. Ct. 564, (1898). Also see discussion of the decision in Commons, J. R., and Andrews, J. B., Principles of Labor Legislation, Rev. ed. 1920, p. 267.

to their interests, while, upon the other hand, certain other classes of persons, particularly those engaged in dangerous or unhealthful employments, have been found to be in need of additional protection."

In sustaining the law as a valid exercise of the police power of the State the court said: "But if it be within the power of a legislature to adopt such means (provisions for proper ventilation, speaking tubes, protection of cages, etc.) for the protection of the lives of its citizens, it is difficult to see why precautions may not also be adopted for the protection of their health and morals. It is as much for the interest of the state that the public health should be preserved as that life should be made secure . . . . While the general experience of mankind may justify us in believing that men may engage in ordinary employments more than eight hours per day without injury to their health, it does not follow that labor for the same length of time is innocuous when carried on beneath the surface of the earth, where the operative is deprived of fresh air and sunlight and is frequently subjected to foul atmosphere and a very high temperature, or to the influence of noxious gases generated by the process of refining or smelting."

The United States Supreme Court in the same decision also sustained the State Supreme Court in the second case which involved labor conditions in smelter and other works wherein ores are reduced and refined.[1]

4. SAFETY AND HEALTH

Prominent among the questions of labor legislation is the one dealing with the conservation of the life and health of wage-earners. As Professor Henderson has well stated, "The nation finds in a sound, strong, and vigorous labor force the physical basis of its power and greatness."[2]

While much may be done by industrial managers, and the private and voluntary efforts of workmen to maintain safety and health in work-places, the conservation of the life, health, and energy of many thousands of wage-earners is too great an undertaking to be left entirely to individual action. It is a question requiring social action; the magnitude and nature of the problem

[1]Holden v. Hardy, 169 U. S. 366, 18 Sup. Ct. 564, (1898).
[2]Henderson, C. R., Citizens in Industry, p. 48.

necessitates state action to afford adequate protection to laborers in work-places.

Control or regulation of conditions surrounding employees in their places of employment, therefore, has been made a subject of legislation in most of the states of the Union; and, we may add, that the statutes enacted relate, in the main to conditions in mines and factories, to transportation, and the erection and repair of buildings.

In Chapter II of this study, attention was given to the steps taken in Utah during the territorial period to safeguard the life and health of wage-earners. In the period of statehood, we find an expansion of these measures looking to the safety and welfare of workers.

As the industrial life of the state has gradually become more highly organized, more careful attention has been given to the matter of the working conditions of wage-earners. Labor organizations, active officials in the State Bureau of Labor and citizen organizations of many kinds have urged the legislature to enact safety and health measures for the benefit of employees, especially in mines. Several serious accidents,[1] also, in coal mines have brought the question of safety in work-places forcibly to the attention of lawmakers.

The most important legal provisions enacted in the State in reference to safety and health problems relate to the welfare of miners. Working underground subject to artificial light, explosive dusts, variations of temperature makes mining an extraordinary hazardous occupation for workmen. For this reason elaborate requirements are stipulated in the laws covering such questions as ventilation, exits, setting and firing of blasts, use of safety lamps, storing of powder, placing of timbers, use of speaking tubes, operation of cages as well as providing for the general inspection and supervision of mines.

a. THE ACT OF 1896

The law passed in 1896[2] provides in detail the safety regulations to be observed in mining operations. It reflects, also, a

---

[1]Orson F. Whitney in his book, entitled, "The Making of a State," p. 283, gives the following account of a mine accident: "Carbon County was the scene of a terrible tragedy in May, 1900, when an accidental explosion in the coal mines at Winter Quarters, near Scofield, killed about two hundred miners, mostly foreigners. It was the most disastrous event of its kind in the history of Utah."

[2]Utah, Laws 1896, C. 113.

desire on the part of the legislature to carry out the provision of the state constitution in regard to the enacting of laws looking to the safety and health of employees in mines.[1]

Briefly stated the main provisions of the law of 1896 are as follows:

(a) The appointment of a coal mine inspector.

(b) Detailed maps to be furnished to the inspector showing all workings and openings in mines.

(c) A sufficient number of escapement shafts to be provided. At least two distinct outlets, as means of ingress and egress, available for persons employed in a coal mine.

(d) Adequate ventilation—every coal mine at a depth of 100 feet or more to be provided with not less than 300 cubic feet of pure air per minute for each person at work, and 300 cubic feet for each animal used therein. The same to be forced through the mine by proper appliances or machinery to dilute or render harmless obnoxious or poisonous gases.

(e) Speaking tubes to be provided, in the various shafts or slopes of a coal mine where persons are lowered or hoisted by machinery, so that conversation may be carried on through the same.

(f) In shaft mines approved safety cages to be provided.

(g) Traveling ways to be provided at the bottom of each shaft which shall enable persons to pass the shaft without having to go under the cage.

(h) Reporting of accidents in mines required. State officials to furnish employers with blanks which call for information relating to the time, place, cause, and nature of the accident, the name of the injured employee, and the like.

(i) Penalty—Violation of the act was punishable by a fine of not less than $300, or more than $500.

(j) Exemptions—The act applied only to mines where six or more men were employed.

b. THE ACTS OF 1901 AND 1903

The act just described was followed, in 1901 and 1903, by a series of measures relating to mines.

The first act of 1901[2] related to the storage and transportation of explosives. Dangerous acids, chemicals or explosives,

---

[1]The State Constitution of Utah, Art. 16, Sec. 6.
[2]Utah, Laws 1921, C. 77.

inflammable substances were to be plainly marked indicating the nature of the package before delivery to a common carrier company, or warehouse, or storehouse.

Violation of this law was punishable by a fine, or imprisonment. The fine not to exceed $300, and the imprisonment not to exceed six months.

The second measure of 1901[1] had reference to fire protection in mines. A mine having but one exit covered by a building containing a mechanical plant was to have fire protection, and where water was not available chemical fire extinguishers were required.

Failure to comply with the act was made a misdemeanor.

The third act, passed the same year,[2] prescribed safety cages in mines. A cage was to be iron bonnetted as a protection from debris, as well as contain devices to hold the cage loaded at any depth to which shafts were sunk.

The penalty for failure to comply with the act was a fine of not less than $200, or more than $300.

These acts were supplemented in the next session of the legislature, held in 1903, by a number of safety measures, relating to the storage of powder, the use of explosives, and the location of powder houses.

The first measure of 1903[3] made it unlawful and punishable by a fine of not less than $100, or more than $1000 for any mining company employing ten or more men, to store, at any one time, in shaft houses or under-ground workings, more than enough powder or high explosives needed for the work of any one day.

The second act of 1903[4] required that powder houses were not to be located within 300 feet of any residence or traveled road. A stipulation was further made in the law limiting the amount to 500 barrels of powder or other explosives, to be stored at any one time. This, however, did not apply to any magazines maintained at a mine or stone quarry.

Penalty for non-compliance with the act was a misdemeanor.

A third enactment passed in 1903[5] made it a felony, punishable by a fine of not more than $5000, or imprisonment not to exceed two years, or both, for any person or company to sell any

[1]Utah, Laws 1901, C. 128.
[2]Utah, Ibid., C. 129.
[3]Utah, Laws 1903, C. 12.
[4]Utah, Laws 1903, C. 76.
[5]Ibid., C. 139.

explosives containing nitro-glycerine, unless each package was
plainly stamped to show the contents of the same.

(1) ACCIDENTS

The Act of 1901,[1] entitled, "Coal Mines", referred principally
to the duties of the mining inspector, a subject which will be
treated in connection with the enforcement of the law, but Section 8 provided that every mine must have stretchers on hand
for convenient use in case any employee was injured in and about
his employment, and Section 13, of the same act, prescribed that
the mining inspector be notified of all accidents.

The Act of 1907,[2] entitled, "Care of Persons Injured in Mines",
stipulated that all mines in Utah, employing ten or more men,
must keep readily accessible a stretcher, blankets, towels and
bandages, liniment, carbolic acid, etc., for the comfort and treatment of injured employees.

Neglect or failure to comply with the law was a misdemeanor
punishable by a fine of not less than $300, or imprisonment for
six months, or both.

(2) PROHIBITION OF DANGEROUS SUBSTANCES IN INDUSTRY

To safe-guard industrial workers, a number of countries have
prohibited the use of substances which render employment ex-
tremely dangerous. A noteworthy example of this prohibitive
method is in the banishing of poisonous phosphorous from the
match industry.

Prohibitory legislation was passed by our Federal Government
in 1912[3] in regard to the use of this substance in the match industry, and the national prominence given to this matter by the
Federal investigation of 1910 led various states, likewise, to
forbid the use of white phosphorous in match factories.

One year after the Federal action referred to in the above
statement, Utah passed a law[4] prohibiting the manufacture and
sale of white phosphorous matches popularly known as "parlor
matches."

[1]Utah, Laws 1901, C. 85.
[2]Utah, Laws 1907, C. 33.
[3]"Congress placed a prohibitory tax of 2 cents a hundred on matches
containing white phosphorus, and prohibited their import or export."
(Commons, J. R., and Andrews, J. B., Principles of Labor Legislation,
Rev. ed. p. 355.)
[4]Utah, Laws 1913, C. 38.

Failure to comply with the act was punishable by a fine of not less than $5 nor more than $25 for the first offense, and a fine of not less than $25 for each subsequent offense.

(3) FACTORIES AND WORKSHOPS

The work done along safety lines in factories and workshops has resulted largely from the activities of the State Industrial Commission in administering the workmen's compensation act.

Rules and regulations having the force of law have been adopted by the Commission, and the same printed and distributed to the factories and other places where necessary.

A factory inspector was appointed by the Commission to inspect all plants[1] and to make recommendations for the proper safeguarding of machinery, and in matters relating to sanitary conditions, ventilation, light, etc.

(4) TRANSPORTATION

Utah has several measures regulating working conditions in transportation.

A law was passed in 1901,[2] which required street railway companies to provide enclosures to protect employees from exposure to inclement weather. These inclosures, or vestibule platforms, to be used during the winter months.

Failure to comply with the act was made a misdemeanor, punishable by a fine of not less than $30 or more than $250 for each offense.

A second law passed in 1917[3] related to safety appliances for public utilities, principally railways. The Public Utilities Commission was given power by the legislature to require every public utility in the state to install and use appropriate safety appliances in plants, grade crossings, junctions and tracks that promote and safeguard the health and safety of its employees, passengers, and the general public.

(5) ADMINISTRATION

In the early period of statehood, the laws relating to mining operations were enforced by a mine inspector working under the direction of the State Commissioner of Labor. Later, when the

---

[1]See Report of the Industrial Commission of Utah, 1918-1920, pp. 193-199.
[2]Utah, Laws 1901, C. 52.
[3]Utah, Laws 1917, C. 47.

duties of the Commissioner of Labor were taken over by the State Industrial Commission, the Bureau of Mine Inspection was made a part of the inspection department under the direction of the Commission.

The inspection department as now organized consists of six inspectors. Three inspectors for mines, viz.; a chief mine inspector, a coal mine inspector, and a metal mine inspector; and in addition a factory inspector, a boiler and elevator inspector and a labor inspector.

a. MINE INSPECTION

The labor report of the Industrial Commission, published in June 1921, contains an account of the work of the mine inspection department for the period, July 1, 1918 to June 30, 1920.[1]

A summarized statement is as follows:

"1· The answering of inquiries regarding the mineral resources of Utah.

2. Inspection of metal mines.
    (a) General inspection for safety.
    (b) Inspection of fatalities.
    (c) Preparation of metal mine safety orders.
    (d) Analysis of accident and labor data.

3. Inspection of coal mines.
    (a) General inspection of the mines.
    (b) Inspection of fatal accidents.
    (c) Preparation of coal mine safety orders.
    (d) Analysis of production, labor and accident data.

4. Inspection of mills and smelters.

5. Inspection of quarries.

6. Welfare work among employees.
    (a) Cooperation with mine rescue car.
    (b) Publication of Utah Safety Record."

As early as 1896, Utah had a coal mine inspector; and, as mentioned in previous pages a brief set of coal mining laws. While these laws have been quite effective, additional safety orders and regulations came into effect as a result of the workmen's compensation act of 1917. Today, therefore, many coal mining companies have adopted for their own use more stringent rules than required by the state law.

Safety inspection work in metal mines, however, has devel-

[1]Report of the Industrial Commission of Utah, 1918-1920, pp. 202-203.

oped during the last few years, that is to say, since the passage of
the workmen's compensation act in 1917. Prior to that time,
there was no medal mine inspector and practically no laws covering metal mine inspection. In the spring of 1919, Utah adopted
a complete set of safety regulations for metal mines, which, according to the report of the Industrial Commission, "were based
on the recommendations of a National Committee of metal mine
operators."[1]

Since the adoption (by order of the Industrial Commission)
of these so-called "General Safety Orders Covering Under-ground
Metal Mining Operations," there has been a decided improvement
in the safety conditions of these mines; especially in the matter
of guarding trolley wires, and overwinding devices for hoists.
Likewise, provisions have been made to lessen the danger from
dust due to the use of dry drilling machines.[2]

b. FACTORY INSPECTION

In the case of factory plants, the inspector likewise makes
inspection visits and keeps a record of each and every plant in
the state. His report shows,[3] for example, that from October
1919 to June 1920, over five hundred visits were made to different plants and a thorough inspection made as to the proper safe-
guarding of machinery, as well as attention given to the welfare
of employees, the sanitary conditions, ventilation, light, etc., in
work-places.

His report further shows that the management of different
industries manifest a spirit of cooperation with his department,
and seem to appreciate the assistance his department is able to
give along safety lines.

c. BOILER AND ELEVATOR INSPECTION

The inspector of boilers and elevators reports[4] that upward of
three hundred inspections were made from October 1919 to June

---

[1]"The report of the National Committee was published in Bulletin No.
75 of the U. S. Bureau of Mines, and represented the results of over five
years' investigation of the different State metal mining laws and the
general safety needs of the industry," Report of the Industrial Commission
of Utah, 1918-1920, p. 251.

[2]Report of the Industrial Commission of Utah, 1918-1920, p. 252.

[3]See Report of the Industrial Commission of Utah, 1918-1920,
pp. 193-195.

[4]Ibid., pp. 196-197.

1920, and with one or two exceptions his orders have been promptly obeyed by owners and lessees of buildings.

A woman inspector has charge of the department of labor inspection and her duties relate to the inspection of departmental stores, factories, canneries, and other places where women and children are employed. This matter has already been mentioned in some detail in connection with the discussion of the administration of the women and child labor laws.

More will be said in later pages of this study concerning the duties of the Industrial Commission to administer and enforce the labor laws of the State. Suffice it to state here that progress has been made in health and safety matters since the Commission was formed.

Legislators in short and busy sessions are unable to formulate adequate protective measures for work-places. On the other hand, commissioners giving their full time to the administering and enforcing of laws for the protection of life, health, safety and welfare of workers are in a better position to establish standards through administrative orders based on continuing investigations. Especially does a policy of administrative orders become effective when the regulations are worked out with the aid of employers and employees.

The useful work of the Industrial Commission no doubt has been due in great part to its success in gaining the friendly cooperation of workers and employers.

It is the cooperation of all parties concerned which makes safety and health inspection effective.

In this connection, the words of Commons and Andrews are significant: "The experience of the worker, the knowledge of the employer, and the critical constructive ability of the expert are all needed in the formation of effective standards of health and safety and in the enforcement of these standards."[1]

(6) INTERPRETATION OF HEALTH AND SAFETY STATUTES

The basis of the health and safety measures set forth in these pages is the police power of the state. And as a general proposition the power of the state to enact inspection or safety appliance laws can hardly be questioned, for the constitutionality

[1]Commons, J. R., and Andrews, J. B., Principles of Labor Legislation, Rev. ed. 1920, p. 381.

and validity of such enactments have been supported by the decisions of State and Federal Courts.

The United States Supreme Court has laid down the doctrine, in the support of such legislation in the case of Nashville, C. & St. L. Ry. v. Alabama, 128 U. S. 96, 9 Sup. Ct. 28, and as recorded by Lindley D. Clark in his book "The Law of the Employment of Labor," p. 89, that 'It is a principle fully recognized by decisions of the state and federal courts, that wherever there is any business which, either from the products created or the instrumentalities used, there is danger to life or property, it is not only within the power of the states, but it is among their plain duties, to make provision against accidents likely to follow in such business, so that the dangers attending it may be guarded against as far as is practicable.'

In the discussion of hours of labor for workmen the case of Holden v. Hardy was cited in some detail to show that the State Supreme Court upheld mine regulations for the protection of the lives and health of workers, and such legislation was regarded as within the power of the legislature to enact.

5. WORKMEN'S COMPENSATION FOR INDUSTRIAL ACCIDENTS

Previous to the enactment of Utah workmen's compensation law in 1917, the liability of employers for injuries sustained by workmen in their employ was regulated under common law and the so-called "fellow-servant rule."

Under the rule of common law, it was considered the duty of the employer to use reasonable care in protecting his employees against injury while engaged in the performance of their work. This was taken to include the duty to provide a safe place to work and to supply safe tools and appliances.

The fellow-servant law[1] passed in 1896, added little or nothing to the common law rule relative to the duty of the employer as to safe places and appliances, but really weakened the common law liability of employers.

The law entitled "Fellow Servants Defined," reads as follows:

Section 1 of the act designates who are not fellow servants. "All persons engaged in the service of any person, firm, or corporation, foreign or domestic, doing business in this state, who are intrusted by such person, firm, or corporation as em-

[1]Utah, Laws 1896, C. 24.

ployer with authority of superintendence, control, or command of other persons in the employ or service of such employer, or with the authority to direct any other employee in the performance of any duties of such employee, are vice-principals of such employer and are not fellow servants."

Section 2 designates who are fellow servants. "All persons who are engaged in the service of such employer, and who, while so engaged, are in the same grade or service and are working together at the same time and place and to a common purpose, neither of such persons being intrusted by such employer with any superintendence or control over his fellow employees, are fellow servants with each other; provided, that nothing herein contained shall be so construed as to make the employees of such employer fellow servants with other employees engaged in any other department of service of such employer. Employees who do not come within the provisions of this section shall not be considered fellow servants."

In recent years the lawmakers of the state have seen the injustice of throwing the burden of liability for injury and death in industries upon the defenceless working man and his family. A movement, therefore, has been in the direction of compensation legislation, that is, to require employers to pay their workmen compensation for injuries sustained in the course of employment whether the accidents were due to the negligence of employers, their agents, or employees or to the necessary risk or danger inherent in the industry. The amount of compulsory compensation to be regulated according to the nature of the injury.

Governor William Spry in his message to the Utah State Legislature in 1915 recommended a workmen's compensation act. The following is a quotation from his message: "Many of the states of the Union have adopted employers' compensation acts. The experience of the states which have adopted such measures entirely justifies my strong recommendation that legislation covering this important matter be written into our statutes. The beneficial results of such acts wherever adopted have been most pronounced and in the interests of both employer and employee. I urge that such measures as will be fair to all be enacted so to place Utah in line with other states of the Union in this advanced legislation."[1]

Several workmen's compensation bills were introduced in the

---

[1]House Journal, Utah, 1915, p. 45.

twelfth session of the legislature in 1915; one by Senator Rideout and another by Representative Lund, but both met with
considerable opposition at a public hearing held on February
15th at the Hotel Utah.

The objections raised (as given in the Deseret Evening News,
February 16, 1915) were that "Senator Rideout's bill was too
drastic, following the New York law in many particulars, while
Representative Lund's bill was opposed because of the exemptions to farmers and others."

Senator Rideout was present at this meeting and outlined the
features of his bill. "He said that the employers opposed his
measure because the rates were too high and the employees were
not satisfied because the rates were too low."

His bill did not provide for a commission but made "it elective with the employer whether he shall come under its provisions.
Any dispute between the employer and the employee in regard
to an injury or the payment under the schedule of compensation
may be settled by the district court on an order to show cause
instituted by the employee."

"P. L. Williams, attorney for the Oregon Short Line, raised
the question as to whether the act was constitutional.

"George S. McAllister, representing the Manufacturers Association, said that the members of the association were in favor
of a compensation act.

"J. Will Knight, of the Provo Woolen Mills, said that he
feared such legislation would tend to widen the breech between
capital and labor.

"E. B. Critchlow, representing a number of mining companies, urged the appointment of a commission to investigate labor
conditions and the possibilities of a state-administered fund."

The general opinion seemed to be that "a commission ought
to be created to study labor conditions in Utah before any such
legislation was enacted."

This was the course taken by the legislature of Utah in 1915.
It passed a measure,[1] entitled, "An Act to Provide for the Appointment of a Commission to Inquire into the Question of
Employers' Liability and Other Matters, and provide an appro-
priation thereof."

The Law reads as follows:

"Section 1. That the Governor of this State is hereby authorized and directed to appoint a commission to consist of seven

[1]Utah, Laws, 1915, C. 50.

members, as follows: One state Senator, one State Representa-́
tive, two employers of labor, two representatives of labor, and
one attorney-at-law. The duties of the Commission so appointed
shall be to make an inquiry, examination and investigation into
the subject of a direct compensation law or a law affecting the
liability of employers to employees for industrial accidents.

"Section 2. That the members of such Commission shall
serve without compensation, except that each shall be entitled
to his actual and necessary expenses incurred in the performance
of his duties under the provisions of this Act.

"Section 3. That for the purpose of its investigations the
Commission or any member or sub-committee thereof, is hereby
authorized to visit different localities in the State, to send for
persons and papers, to investigate the laws of other States and
countries, to administer oaths and to examine witnesses and
papers respecting all matters pertaining to the subjects referred
to in this Act, to purchase books and supplies and to employ and
pay all necessary assistants.

"Section 4. That the expenses incurred by the Commission,
and its employees shall be paid upon the presentation of proper
itemized vouchers signed by the chairman of the Commission and
approved by the Governor, provided such expenses shall not
exceed five hundred dollars.

"Section 5. That the Commissioner of Immigration, Labor
and Statistics is hereby directed to co-operate with the Commission and to render it any proper aid and assistance by the Bureau
of Immigration, Labor and Statistics, as, in his judgment, will
not interfere with his proper conduct of his department.

"Section 6. The Commission herein authorized to be appointed shall organize by the election of a chairman and secretary and shall submit a full report of its work and findings to
the members and members-elect of the next Legislature at least
sixty days before its next regular session, and shall include
therein its recommendations for legislation, together with such
bill or bills providing for a speedy remedy for employees for injuries received."

Pursuant to the provisions of Section 1 of this law, Governor
William Spry, on March 1, 1916, appointed a Commission, con-
sisting of State Senator, Don B. Colton; State Representative,
Ira R. Browning; Mr. R. C. Gemmel, Mr. H. B. Windsor, Mr. H.
K. Russell, Mr. Charles H. Pearson and Mr. Le Grand Young.
The Commission met and elected the following officers: Senator,

Don B. Colton, Chairman; Mr. Le Grand Young, Vice-Chairman, and Mr. H. B. Windsor, Secretary, and Mr. H. K. Russell, Assistant Secretary.

The Commission held a number of meetings and discussed the compensation laws of various states and several members while on eastern trips visited a number of states and inquired into the workings of their compensation laws. The Commission also interviewed Chairman Mullin of the Nevada State Commission when he was stopping over in Salt Lake, relative to the compensation law of his state. Due, however, to the small means (five hundred dollars) at their command to make their findings and report them, the Commission could not visit other states as a body, to observe, at first hand, the operations of the various laws.

As a result of their investigation[1] of the several compensation laws in force the Commission favored the Statute of Indiana, relative to this subject; and, therefore, used the statute of this state as a basis for its bill to the legislature in 1917.[2]

The Commission was convinced, through its investigation, so far as the principle was concerned, that a workingmen's compensation law is just and far preferable to any employers' liability law. Likewise they were agreed that such a law ought to be placed upon the statute books of Utah.

In order to get the compensation system established a conservative measure was proposed which the Commission thought would be reasonably considerate of all parties and sufficient for initiatory needs.

Six members of the Commission signed the report (which included the proposed bill) submitted to the legislature. One member, Mr. Russell, refused to sign the majority report on the ground that more consideration should be given to working men and women than was accorded them in the proposed measure. He, therefore, submitted a brief report to the legislature setting

[1]The Commission studied in a tentative way, all the laws, and quite thoroughly some of the laws of the different states. The Secretary of the Commission communicated with commissions and officers of the several states, relative to the matter in hand, asking for copies of their compensation laws, and inquiring into the workings thereof.

[2]See Report of the Employer's Liability and Workmen's Compensation Commission, 1917.

forth his objections to the proposed law.   He thought the bill faulty in the following ways: (1) the waiting period (14 days) was too long, and should be reduced to three days; (2) occupational diseases should be included in the measure; (3) provision should be made for a state insurance fund; (4) the compensation schedule should be increased; (5) a provision should be included in the bill dealing with accident prevention.[1*]

When the workmen's compensation bill, drafted by the Commission, was introduced in the legislature in 1917, Governor Simon Bamberger made the following recommendation to the legislature relative to this measure:

"It is well for all of us to remember in the conduct of our official duties one fundamental rule of free government—where property rights and human rights conflict human rights must always prevail.   The interest of the working man, the wageearner, the settler, the home-builder should be the first consideration of every law making body.

"That the rights of the workingman shall be safeguarded I respectfully recommend the passage of a just and equitable workingmen's compensation act.   The legislature in 1915 provided for the creation of a Commission to investigate this subject and report to the present legislature.   This Commission has completed its work and has laid its report before you for your consideration.   You should consider well the work of the Commission and the measure it has submitted for your approval.   It is for the legislature to decide whether or not the draft of this Commission meets the requirements of a just and equitable workingmen's compensation act.   If it does it should be passed. If it does not, it should be so amended as to meet the requirements of such a law.   I respectfully recommend the passage of a compensation act that will protect the rights of both employers and employees and provide a just and reasonable compensation for those injured in the course of their legitimate employment."[2]

[1]See Report of the Employer's Liability and Workmen's Compensation Commission, 1917, pp. 28-35.
[*]Later when the compensation law was amended consideration was given to various recommendations which Mr. Russell set forth in his minority report.
[2]House Journal, Utah, 1917, p. 63.

The provisions of the proposed act were passed by the legislature in 1917[1] with a number of modifications.[2] The digest of the law as passed is set forth in the following pages.[3]

(1) ACT OF 1917 CREATING THE STATE INDUSTRIAL COMMISSION OF UTAH AND PROVIDING FOR WORKMEN'S COMPENSATION

The workmen's compensation law of Utah ranks as one of the most progressive pieces of legislation so far enacted in the state, and perhaps the very best law upon the statute books from labor's standpoint.

On account of the importance of this act it has been deemed advisable to treat the principal provisions of the law in separate units, or divisions. For our purpose the act may be conveniently discussed under four main heads, (1) scope of the law, (2) compensation benefits, (3) compensation insurance, (4) administration.

(a) SCOPE OF THE LAW

The Utah compensation law is compulsory as to all employments except those having less than four employees, farm labor, domestic service, casual labor and those not in the usual course of the employer's business, but optional or voluntary, as to employers having less than four employees. Likewise, the act is compulsory as to all public employees, state, county, and city except elective officials or those receiving a salary over $2,400 a year.[4]

---

[1]Utah, Laws 1917, C .100.

[2]The tentative workmen's compensation law as proposed by the Commission made the waiting period 14 days; the law as passed reduced the waiting period to 10 days. Again, the scale of compensation was increased from 50 to 55 per cent of the employee's weekly wage, and the maximum allowance for partial disability was increased from $3000 to $4500. The weekly maximum allowance was increased from $12 to $15. There was also a slight increase in the amount allowed for medical and surgical and funeral expenses. Another provision of the law as passed was to provide for a State Insurance Fund.

[3]The workmen's compensation law as enacted is featured principally after the compensation laws of California, Indiana, and Ohio. With respect to procedure the Industrial Commission of Utah, administering the law, investigated the system used by the California Industrial Commission, and has in great measure followed the California trend in systematizing its work.

[4]Various states of the Union make similar exclusions in their compensation laws.

For a complete list of the inclusions and exclusions of the compensation laws of the United States (up to December 31, 1917) see, Bulletin No. 240 of the United States Bureau of Labor Statistics, pp. 18-19.

Number of Persons Subject to Compensation Act.—At this point, it may be well to mention the number and per cent of employees affected by the compensation law. These figures are based on the Federal Census of 1910 and therefore do not cover the number of employees at present. They are given here primarily to show to what extent workers are included and excluded from the benefits of the act; and the percentages show, with a reasonable degree of accuracy, the relative status of employees of the state.

On the basis of the United States Census for 1910 Carl Hookstadt estimated (in the Bulletin on Comparison of Workmen's Compensation Laws of the United States up to December 31, 1917) that the total number of employees covered by the Utah compensation act was 59,346 which was 48.6 per cent of the total number gainfully employed and 73.1 per cent of the total number of employees.

On the other hand, the number of employees not covered by the act was 21,839, or 17.9 per cent of the total number gainfully employed and 26.9 per cent of the total number of employees.[1]*

The report of the State Industrial Commission for the period July 1917 to June 1918, page 149, mentions that about 72,740 wage-earners in the State of Utah were at that time covered by the workmen's compensation act.

Suits for Damage.—The act enumerates the conditions under which employees are allowed to bring actions at law: (1) If employer fails to insure his risk when injury is caused by neglect or default of employer. In such action, the defenses of the fellow-servant rule, assumption of risk, and contributory negligence are abrogated; (2) if injury causes death, defenses are allowed and employer's negligence must be proved; (3) if injury is due to employer's willful misconduct and such act indicates a willful disregard of the life and bodily safety of employees. In

---

[1]See Bulletin, No. 240, United States Bureau of Labor Statistics, 1917, pp. 28-33.

*Mr. Carl Hookstadt in ascertaining the number of persons subject to compensation acts, first deducted the employers from the number gainfully employed as reported by the census, "the remainder being the bona fide employees or wage-earners; from the latter group were then excluded those employees exempted by the provisions of the law as interpreted by the court or commission of the state." He points out, however, that it was difficult, "and in some cases impossible, to apply the census classifications to those of the compensation acts." (See Bulletin No. 240 United States Bureau of Labor Statistics, page 27.)

these cases, the injured employee may elect whether to accept compensation or sue for damages, but he may not do both.

Special Contract.—The law also makes provisions in regard to special contracts. In order to secure for the employee the compensation benefits contemplated by the act he is forbidden to waive his rights and accept from his employer benefits which are not equivalent to those provided by the law. Substitute systems of insurance may be approved if benefits equal those of the act.

Injuries Covered.—As already noted the compensation law is limited as to employments covered and persons compensated and it is also limited as to injuries covered. In fact no state of the Union compensates for all injuries, irrespective of the conditions under which they occur.[1] The rule in most of the States is to grant compensation only for injuries which "arise out of" and "in the course of" employment.[2] Again, in the vast majority of states compensation is denied for injuries occasioned in whole or in part through some gross negligence or fault of the employee.

[1]See Bulletin No. 240, United States Bureau of Labor Statistics, p. 43, for a detailed table of the compensation laws of the several states classified according to injuries covered and conditions under which injuries are compensable and noncompensable.

[2]In the above mentioned Bulletin (No. 240, p. 46) is an extract of a definition given by the Massachusetts Supreme Court of an injury which arises "in the course of" and "out of" employment. It reads as follows: . . . . 'It is sufficient to say that an injury is received "in the course of" employment, when it comes while the workman is doing the duty which he is employed to perform. It arises "out of" the employment, when there is apparent to the rational mind, upon consideration of all the circumstances, a casual connection between the conditions under which the work is required to be performed and the resulting injury. Under this test, if the injury can be seen to have followed as a natural incident of the work, and to have been contemplated by a reasonable person familiar with the whole situation as a result of the exposure occasioned by the nature of the employment then it arises "out of" the employment. But it excludes an injury which can not fairly be traced to the employment as a contributing proximate cause and which comes from a hazard to which the workman would have been equally exposed apart from the employment. The causative danger must be peculiar to the work and not common to the neighborhood; it must be incident to the character of the business and not independent of the relation of master and servant. It need not have been foreseen or expected, but after the event it must appear to have had its origin in the risk connected with the employment and to have flowed from that source as a rational consequent.' For a fuller account of the case giving rise to the above statement see McNichol v. Employers' Liability Assurance Association, 215 Mass. 497.

Under the Utah law an injury by accident arising out of and in the course of employment is compensable. Compensation, however, is withheld if the injury is intentionally or purposely self-inflicted. Industrial or occupational diseases are likewise excluded from the benefits of the act.

Waiting Period.—Another factor must also be noted in connection with a compensable injury, that is, the degree of severity of the injury or the duration of disability caused by it. In most states, no compensation is allowed for the first few days after the injury, and this noncompensable period at the beginning of disability is generally known as the "waiting period."[1]

The Utah law follows this customary plan and allows no monetary benefit for the first ten days after the date of injury, except the disbursement for medical aid and funeral expenses in case of fatal injuries.

(b) COMPENSATION BENEFITS

Probably the next primary factor of a compensation law, after the consideration of its scope is that of compensation benefits. This includes such important features as the compensation scale, the period for which compensation is paid, the maximum and minimum payments, the amount of medical service provided as well as the time limit for which to make claims.

It was pointed out in the discussion of the old system of employers' liability that the payment of damages to an injured employee was based upon the employer's fault or negligence (the common law principle). The new compensation system has, in the main, abolished the theory of negligence and finds its justification in the principle of economic necessity. As Carl Hookstadt has tersely stated: "Instead of the least able unit of industry assuming its risks, the consuming public, acting through the employer, furnishes relief to injured workers by fixed awards."[2]

The compensation laws of the several states frequently vary as to the extent to which an injured employee should be compensated for losses sustained as a result of injury. As an aid, to determine the proper amounts to be awarded, the general plan

---

[1]The waiting period is generally about ten days or two weeks. There is now, however, a tendency on the part of States to reduce the waiting period. Oregon and Porto Rico have no waiting period at all, but allow compensation for injuries producing any disability.

[2]See Bulletin No. 240, United States Bureau of Labor Statistics, p. 49.

has been to classify compensation benefits according as they apply to death, total disability and partial disability, together with provision for permanent and temporary disability. In addition the laws usually provide for medical service and burial expenses in case of fatal injuries.

Scale.—The compensation scale, as a rule, is based on the earning capacity of the injured employee at the time of injury and the award ranges from 50 to 66⅔ per cent of his weekly or monthly wages, within certain maximum limits. A further limitation is also usually made in regard to the total compensation allowed as well as stipulating the maximum period of compensation.

Under the Utah law, compensation is based upon wages. The compensation is 55 per cent of the employee's weekly wages, but within certain limits as the following account will show.

Compensation for Temporary Disability.—In case of temporary total disability, the employee is allowed 55 per cent of his weekly wage so long as such disability is total, but not to exceed $12, and not less than $7 per week. The total sum received must not exceed $4,500, nor cover a period of more than six years.

Compensation for Partial Disability.—Where the injury causes partial disability, the employee receives 55 per cent of the difference between his wages before the accident and the amount he is able to earn thereafter. The maximum amount must not exceed $12 a week. The following account shows the number of weeks for which compensation is payable for specified injuries. The list of injuries mentioned is a partial one, and does not cover all cases which are compensable. It is given to show the nature of partial disabilities and the maximum period of compensation.

For loss of:

One arm	200 weeks
One hand	150 weeks
One thumb	30 weeks
One index finger	20 weeks
One middle finger	15 weeks
One third finger	12 weeks
One little finger	9 weeks
One leg	150 weeks
One foot	125 weeks
One great toe	15 weeks
One other toe	6 weeks
Sight of one eye	100 weeks

In the complete list of partial disabilities specified by the law a subdivision occurs in a number of the specified injuries mentioned. For example, for the loss of one arm at or near the shoulder, compensation is paid 200 weeks; one arm at the elbow, the compensation is for 180 weeks; and one arm between the wrist and the elbow, the period of compensation is for 160 weeks.

Compensation for Total Disability.—For permanent total disability, the disabled workman receives 55 per cent of his weekly wage for five years from date of injury, and thereafter 40 per cent for life. The compensation must not be more than $15, nor less than $7 per week.

In Section 78 of the law, a total disability is defined as follows: "The loss of both legs, or both eyes, or any two thereof, shall constitute total and permanent disability, to be compensated according to the provisions of this section."

Compensation for Death.—If the injury results in death, the following benefits are allowed: (1) when there are no dependents, burial expenses (maximum $150) are paid by the employer or insurance carrier, and the sum of $750 must also be paid into the State Insurance Fund Treasury, unless the employer is insured in this fund; (2) dependent persons (a wife and minor child) are granted 55 per cent of the weekly wage for a period of six years, but not to exceed the maximum of $15, nor amount to more than $4,500, or less than $2,000.

In other cases where there are partly dependent persons similar benefits are allowed for a period of six years or for such a period as the Commission may in each case determine.

Medical Service.—The Utah law provides for medical, nurse and hospital services and medicines for injured employees, but not to exceed the sum of $200—the same to be paid by employer or insurance carrier. Furthermore, the State Industrial Commission has power to adopt rules and regulations with respect to the furnishing, and payment therefore, of medical, nurse and hospital service and medicine to injured employees entitled thereto.

Time for Notice and Claim.—Workmen compensation laws often place limitations on the time of giving notice and for presenting claims under the act. Notice as to injury is usually required within from 10 to 30 days, and claims for disability and death, within from 6 months to 2 years. In the Utah law, the time for notice and claim is fixed by the Industrial Commission.

(c) COMPENSATION INSURANCE

Compensation awards are attained through a system of insurance, and the cost of compensation is borne by employers.

To safeguard employees from insolvency or other contingencies which occasionally might happen to employers, provision is made for security of compensation payments. Employers must insure in the State Fund or private companies or provide self-insurance. The private companies authorized to transact workmen's compensation insurance are subject to the rules and regulations of the State Industrial Commission, and where employers are authorized to carry their own insurance, they are required to furnish the Commission satisfactory proof of solvency and financial ability to pay direct the compensation in amount and manner described in the law.

State Insurance Fund.—While employers may maintain their own insurance, or insure in private companies, the state of Utah also maintains a fund in competition with the other two systems. The fund is under the management of the Industrial Commission and based upon the same principles and subject to the same general requirements as those governing Mutual Insurance Companies. A contract or policy is issued to every employer in the State Insurance Fund and the premiums are paid over to the State Treasurer, custodian of the Fund.

While the period of operation of the State Fund has been short it would seem, from reports of the Industrial Commission, and according to the report of the State Commissioner of Insurance for the year 1920, to have been extraordinarily successful.

The last report of the Commission shows that the net premiums of the state fund for three years, July 1, 1917 to June 30, 1920, amounted to $563,663.33. For the same period the benefits paid amounted to $138,523.03. For the third year 1919-1920, the State Insurance Fund wrote $209,009.73. This represents about 25 per cent of the business of insurance carriers so far as it applies to workmen's compensation insurance.

The Utah fund had, on June 30, 1920, assets of $423,135.87, which cover all liabilities and leaves a surplus fund of $134,406.79.

The assets are safely and profitable invested in high-class public securities.

The report further shows that claimants are given prompt and equitable consideration, and that dividends of $32,814.89

were paid on the first two years' business. The third year (1920) the multiplier was reduced from the stock company basis of 2.72 to the fund basis of 2.24 with a saving to policyholders for the third year of about $44,700.[1]

Insurance Companies.—In respect to stock companies or mutual associations transacting the business of workmen's compensation insurance the law requires stock companies to have an aggregate capital and surplus of $600,000, that is, paid up capital stock of $500,000 and a surplus of $100,000. Mutual insurance companies are required to possess net assets over and above liabilities of $600,000. Likewise the reserves in both cases must be 65 per cent of the annual premiums.

The labor organizations of Utah favor state insurance. This view is taken on the ground that workmen's compensation insurance is primarily a matter of public welfare into which the question of profits of an intermediary agent should not be allowed to enter. They further contend that under a system of state insurance employers get insurance at a minimum cost and because of reduced costs of insurance premiums employees get greater benefits. The opposite view taken by private insurance carriers is that the entrance of the state into this field of enterprise is unwarranted and undesirable. They contend that workmen's compensation insurance should be left to carefully supervised companies of unquestioned responsibility, rather than the state to enter into private business of this character.

(d) ADMINISTRATION

The administrative feature of the compensation acts of the several states assumes two general types; the commission, or board type; and the self-administrative or court type. The commission system, however,, is the one provided for in most of the states. The Utah law provides for a commission of three members to enforce the law, including the administration of the State Insurance Fund. In fact, this commission administers the entire body of labor laws of the state.

Settlement of Compensation Claims.—The settlement of compensation cases is one of the principal functions of the Industrial Commission. It is given full power to determine all questions relating to compensation. The disposition it makes of

[1] Report of the Industrial Commission of Utah, July 1, 1918, to June 10, 1920, pp. 41-46.

cases is final and conclusive on questions of fact. Right of appeal from the Commission's rulings to the Supreme Court is limited to questions of law only.

Revision of Benefits.—The Commission is allowed to modify at any time, former findings if circumstances justify a change. On its own motions it is also given the privilege when deemed advisable to commute periodical benefits to lump sum settlements.

Formal Hearings.—Compensation cases are generally settled without the necessity of formal hearings before the Commission. Such cases as come before the Commission for formal hearings are those where controversies have arisen between the employee and employer, or insurance carrier.

Accident Reporting.—The Utah law requires all employers to report all accidents, fatal or otherwise, to the Commission within one week after occurrence of an accident resulting in personal injury, that is, accidents to employees arising out of or in the course of their employment.

Accident Prevention.—The Utah law leaves the question of safety work to the Industrial Commission.[1*]

(2) UTAH'S AMENDED WORKMEN'S COMPENSATION LAW OF 1919

While compensation legislation is rather generally accepted throughout the entire country,[2] it is still in a developmental stage, and additions and changes are made in existing statutes from year to year.[3]

Amendatory legislation was made in the Utah workmen's compensation law in 1919.[4] The term of the Industrial Com-

---

[4]Carl Hoodstadt states that compensation enactments have given an impetus to accident prevention work. (United States Bulletin No. 240, p. 92.)

*Professor E. A. Ross points out that, "the happiest result of a workingman's compensation law is not that injured workingmen get something, but that employers anticipating their new liabilty, greatly reduce the number of accidents by adopting safety measures and devices." (Ross, E. A., The Principles of Sociology, p. 633.)

[2]From 1911 to 1920, a period of nine years, 42 of the 48 states as well as Porto Rico and the two Territories of Alaska and Hawaii, had adopted compensation laws. The six states without compensation laws were Arkansas, Florida, Georgia, Mississippi, North Carolina, South Carolina. (See, 6th ed. of Pamphlet issued by American Association for Labor Legislation, Standard for Workmen's Compensation Laws, Revised January 1, 1920.)

[3]See Monthly Labor Review, U. S. Dept. of Labor, Vol. 12, No. 1, pp. 167-170.

[4]Utah, Laws 1919, C. 63.

missioners was changed from four to six years. The act was also extended in its scope from employers of four or more employees to employers of three or more. The scale of compensation increased from 55 to 60 per cent of wages, and the award paid after five years' disability from 40 to 45 per cent. The maximum weekly allowance from $12 to $15, and the minimum for permanent total disability was made the same as for temporary disability, that is, not less than $7 a week.

The total compensation payable for temporary and permanent partial and death cases was increased from $4,500 to $5,000. Compensation for specific injuries made additional to benefits for temporary total disability. The waiting period which had formerly been ten days was now reduced to three, and allowance for medical and surgical aid increased from $200 to $500. Further change was also made in regard to where an employee who had previously incurred a permanent partial disability, incurs a subsequent permanent partial disability so that the compensation payable for his combined injuries is greater than the compensation which except for the pre-existing disability would have been payable for the latter injury, the employer is made liable for the latter injury only, and the remainder of the benefits due is to be paid out of the special fund composed of the $750 payments which employers are required to make whenever one of their employees was killed leaving no dependents. Strict conditions are also prescribed for insurance companies desiring to write workmen's compensation business, and the State Insurance Fund was given power to insure employers against liability claims as well as compensation claims, claims against employers who had failed to insure, instead of being made liquidate claims for damages, are made leins against the employer's real property.

(3) AMENDATORY LEGISLATION OF 1921

The amendments made in 1921[1] to the compensation law of Utah relate in the main to procedure rather than to substantive changes in the scope of the law.

The Commission is given wider option in administering the law. In its discretion it is given authority to increase medical and hospital benefits above the standard of $500 named in the law if "it shall find that in particular cases such an amount is insufficient," likewise a similar enlargement is allowed in regard

[1]Utah, Laws 1921, C. 67.

to burial expenses from that named in the law of $150. It may also extend payments indefinitely to beneficiaries, (taking into consideration "all reasonable circumstances") who are in a dependent condition at the termination of the period for which benefits have been awarded under the act.

Another power granted the Commission is to fix the fees of attorneys employed in cases coming before the Commission.

A new provision makes benefits to beneficiaries, residing outside of the United States or its dependences, or Canada, one-half the amount provided by the law.

Another change makes a modification in the provision establishing a minimum benefit of $7 a week. Where wages are less than $7, the wages earned is the amount of compensation.

The provision of the act relating to the right to sue in case of fatal injuries is repealed and compensation is made the exclusive remedy where the law is applicable.[1]

In case of death of employee with no dependents the employer or the insurance carrier, in lieu of the payment of $750 in to the State treasury, may pay an amount equal to 20 per cent of the death benefit payable in cases where wholly dependent persons survive.

.A new section prescribes a penalty of 15 per cent reduction in compensation where an employee fails to give notice (within 48 hours) to his employer of an injury or fails to report for medical treatment within the time prescribed.

(4) CONSTITUTIONALITY

A number of cases have been decided by the Supreme Court of Utah relative to the constitutionality of the workmen's compensation law. While it may not be necessary to mention all these cases it seems advisable to give a brief statement of the court's rulings in a number of cases.

In April, 1918, the case of the Industrial Commission of Utah

---

[1]Section 5, Article 16, of the Constitution of the State of Utah which provides that "right of action to recover damage for injuries resulting in death, shall never be abrogated, and the amount recoverable shall not be subject to any statutory limitation" was amended (by vote of the people in 1920) to read as follows:

"The right of action to recover damages for injuries resulting in death, shall never be abrogated, and the amount recoverable shall not be subject to any statutory limitation, except in cases where compensation for injuries resulting in death is provided for by law." This amendment was necessary for the efficient operation of the laws governing compensation insurance.

v. Daly Mining Co., 51 U. 602, arose over the question of compulsory compensation. The Commission had applied for a writ of mandate to compel the Daly Mining Company to furnish security for payment of compensation to employees.

Section 53 of the compensation act provides, "Employers . . . . shall secure compensation to their employees in one of the following ways: (a) by the state insurance; (b) by insurance with an insurance company; (c) by a deposit of securities"

While employers may elect one of three ways to secure the payment of compensation to which their employees may become entitled under the act, the court held that the legislature had manifestly intended this provision to be mandatory and not merely permissive. Very little, if anything would be gained by the enactment of the law, the court said, if this feature of the act was elective.

A citation of cases[1] was made by the court to show that numerous decisions of the Supreme Courts of various States as well as decisions of the Supreme Court of the United States sustained this view.

By a unanimous decision the court sustained the power of the commission to compel the Daly Mining Company to comply with its orders.

The case of, Utah Copper Co. v. Industrial Commission 193 Pac. 24, involved a number of questions, but the principal one was a consideration of a provision of the State Constitution which declares that "the right of action to recover damages for injuries resulting in death shall never be abrogated, and the amount recoverable shall not be subject to any statutory limitation." (Art. 16, Sec. 3.)

The claimant was a widow. Her husband had lost his life while working on an irrigation canal. The defendant made the claim that the nature of the work was classed as casual by the company. The Commission and the court took the view that the work was so intimately connected with the business of the

[1]Cases cited:
State ex. rel. v. Clausen, 65 Washington 156, 117 Pac. 1101, 37 L. R. A. (N. S.) 466.
State v. Mountain Timber Co., 75 Washington 518, 135 Pac. 645, L. R. A. 1917 D. 10.
Mountain Timber Co. v. Washington 243 U. S. 219, 37 Sup. Ct. 240, 61 L. Ed. 685, Ann. Cas. 1917 D. 612.
New York Cent. R. Co. v. White, 243 U. S. 188, 37 Sup. Ct. 247, 61 L. Ed. 667 L. R. A. 1917 D. 1. Ann. Cas. 1917 D. 629.

employer as to form a part of the regular employment. Again, the defendant raised the question of the rights of a self-insurer but the court pointed out that an insurance carrier was bound by the act to the findings of the Commission as determined in cases of claims for awards.

The principal contention, however, seemed to be the one based upon the provision of the State Constitution as cited above. There was an unborn child at the date of hearing, and the defendant tried to show that its rights could not be precluded in the action of the Commission. Therefore it was claimed that the company would be exposed to double liability which would be taking its property without due process of law.

The compensation law in view of the constitutional restriction mentioned gives to the dependants of employees fatally injured the option of suit at law to recover damages or to accept benefits under the act, but the acceptance of benefits stands as a bar to suit. The court held, therefore, that the election of the award by the widow was a valid waiver of all rights by suit at law.

The case of Utah Fuel Co. v. Industrial Commission 194 Pac. 122, was based upon the question of the administrative power of the Commission which it was claimed violates the provision as to due process of law.

The court upheld the right of the Commission to make awards in disputed cases. To hold otherwise, the court said, would be to require the Commission to dismiss cases in which there was dispute in regard to claims. This in turn would defeat the purpose of the act which aims to secure compensation for injury received in the course of employment without the delay, costs, and annoyance of a suit at law. This view was said to be "predicated on the police power inherent in every sovereignty, the power to legislate and govern for the best interests of the state."

(5) OPERATION OF UTAH'S WORKMEN'S COMPENSATION LAW

The first annual report of the State Industrial Commission for the year ending June 30, 1918, states that 11,872 injuries were reported. Of this number 11,663 were temporary, 109 permanent partial, and 90 fatalities. The number of injuries reported for the fiscal year ending June 30, 1919, was 8,884 of which 8,718 were temporary, 95 permanent partial, 3 permanent total, and 73 fatalities. For the fiscal year ending June 30, 1920, the total number was 10,183 of which 9,958 were temporary, 126 permanent partial, and 99 fatalities.

The total compensation paid in 1918 including the medical cost was $232,667.08. Of this amount, $109,221 was paid for temporary injuries and $30,763.38 for permanent partial injuries and $24,572.10 to dependents of those meeting with injuries causing death. The total cost for medical services, nursing, hospital care, medicine and funeral expenses was $68,110.60.

The total compensation and medicinal cost, in 1919, was $419,181.58. Of this amount $117,850 was paid for temporary injuries, and $63,048.00 for medical services in connection with these injuries. The compensation and medical cost for permanent partial was $72,096.98, and the total death cost was $166,186.60.

The total number of days lost due to the 8,718 temporary injuries was 103,878.

For the fiscal year ending June 30, 1920, the total amount paid in all cases was $632,037.71.[1]

6. FIREMEN'S FUND

In addition to the mothers' pension law and the workmen's compensation act, mention may also be made of the act of 1911[2] creating a fund for firemen.

The chief of the Salt Lake Fire Department and other members of the department were active in getting his bill before the legislature. It was considered right and just that firemen worn out in the service should receive some compensation in their reclining years.[3]

This law applies to all fire insurance companies doing business in any incorporated city or town in the state or an organized fire department under control of a mayor or city council with equipment and apparatus amounting to $500 or more.

Premiums.—One per cent of the amount of all premiums of fire insurance is to be turned over to the State Insurance Commissioner, and the money so collected placed in the hands of the State Treasurer as a fund out of which to pay benefits to the heirs of deceased firemen or to disabled firemen.

[1]Report of the Industrial Commission of Utah, July 1, 1917 to June 30, 1918, p. 149, and Report, Industrial Commission of Utah, July 1, 1918 to June 30, 1920, pp. 135-136.
[2]Utah, Laws 1911, C. 146.
[3]Letter from E. H. Thorn—Secretary, Salt Lake City Fire Department.

Benefits.—Every person of a regularly organized fire department, as described, is entitled to benefits on the following conditions: (1) for the loss of life while in the performance of duties devolving upon him as such there is paid to his heirs the sum of $2500; (2) for an injury received in the performance of his duties, resulting in dismemberment of hands and feet, the sum of $2500; one hand and one foot, $2500; one hand or one foot, $1,250; loss of both eyes, $2,500; and the loss of one eye, $1,250.

Penalty.—Failure to meet the requirement of the law is punishable by a fine of $100 for each day payment is delayed.

Amended Act of 1919.—In 1919,[1] the Act of 1911, establishing the Firemen's Pension Fund was amended. The premium set aside for the fund was now made 25 per cent of the annual tax collected upon fire insurance companies within the state.

Pension Rate.—The act includes all paid firemen in service, and a fireman performing twenty years active service in a regularly constituted fire department, and who has reached the age of sixty years, may at his option, retire from active service and receive a monthly pension for the remainder of his life. The pension is to be one half of his monthly salary at the time of his retirement, but not to exceed $100 a month. For injury, the benefit is to be made in accordance with the provisions of the workmen's compensation act. In case of death, his dependents, if there be any, are allowed $2,000.

Amended Act of 1921.—The act of 1919 was also slightly amended in 1921,[2] making a more definite provision for firemen who had performed twenty years of active service, but who had not reached the age of sixty years. If physically or mentally incapicated for further service said firemen were eligible to the pension allowance granted to retiring firemen.

7. POLICE DEPARTMENT PENSIONS

In the last session of the legislature, held in the early months of the year (1921) a measure[3] was enacted to provide pensions for employees of police departments in cities of first and second class.

A person is eligible for the pension who has reached the age of sixty years and upwards and who has performed service for

[1]Utah, Laws 1919, C. 46.
[2]Utah, Laws 1921, C. 53.
[3]Utah, Laws 1921, C. 12.

twenty years in a police department in one of such cities. Fifteen years of this time must be in the continuous service of the police department next prior to reaching such age. The rate of pension is $30.00 a month so long as any such person may live, the same to be paid by the city retiring any such person.

It was mainly through the efforts of the Salt Lake City Police Mutual Aid Association that this law was enacted.

8. FRATERNAL INSURANCE

A law enacted in 1911,[1] regulates the activities of private societies in the matter of mutual benefits to their members. These private associations may be organized with seven or more persons, the majority of whom are citizens of the state. They are likewise allowed to provide death benefits as well as benefits for temporary and permanent physical disability either as result of accident, disease, or old age.

[1] Utah, Laws 1911, C. 148.

CHAPTER VI

SUNDRY STATUTES

1. RESTRICTIONS ON EMPLOYEES AND GROUNDS FOR SUCH RESTRICTIONS

Lindley Clark, in his book, entitled, "The Law of the Employment of Labor," p. 108, has pointed out that, "The conditions and requirements of certain occupations are such that the welfare of fellow workmen, or of the public, or of both, is dependent on the experience and technical ability of the employee."

Possibly it may be well to say a word here concerning the grounds for the enactment of laws placing restrictions on employees. In this connection, probably we can do no better than to quote the words of Mr. Lindley Clark. He writes:

". . . . . . How far such laws may properly go is indeed a question not yet decided, nor is it easy of decision. . . . . .

"In the case of barbers there is usually coupled with the question of skill that of personal freedom from contagious and infectious diseases . . . . . . so that there is here clearly in view the protection of the public health . . . . . Within the range of health provisions these laws command support under the police power of the state[1] . . . .

"The entire subject of examination and licensing, as is true of the whole subject of the regulation of the conditions of employment, is affected by the development of industry in its modern forms, and the corresponding growth of ideas of public policy. The contractor for work no longer does it himself, and neither fellow servants nor the employer are able to observe and guard against the negligent acts of unskilled workmen as may easily have been the case in days of small undertakings and intimate relationships between workmen and employer . . . The law indicates to the individual a standard that has been fixed upon as the result of the collective experience of the many . . . . and it cannot be questioned that the condition of both employer and employee is the better for such provisions. The fact remains

[1]See State v. Briggs, 45 Ore. 366, 77 Pac. 750.

that a just ground for intervention must appear, and that the rights of liberty and property may not be arbitrarily infringed upon under the guise of either health or safety regulations."[1]

(1) COAL MINE INSPECTOR

It has been the policy of the State of Utah to require coal mine inspectors to have certain qualifications for their positions. The statute passed in 1896,[2] for example, required a coal mine inspector to furnish a bond of $5,000 for the faithful performance of his duties, and a further provision in this act required that a coal-mine inspector be a practical coal miner with five years experience.

(2) BARBERS

In the case of barbers, the public is affected; and therefore, measures have been enacted regulating the practice of barbering. In 1903,[3] a law was passed which provides for the appointment of a board of three examiners charged with the duty of adopting rules and regulations covering sanitary requirements of barber shops. This board also holds examinations[4] at certain times and grants certificates to those who have studied this occupation for a period of one year as an apprentice or in a barber school, and who is above sixteen years of age and free from contagious and infectious diseases.

Violation of the law is a misdemeanor punishable by a fine of not less than $10 nor more than $100, or by imprisonment for not less than ten days nor more than ninety days.

Several amendments have been made to this law, one in 1907,[5] another in 1915,[6] and one in 1919,[7] and the last in 1921.[8]

These amendments, however, made only slight changes in the law of 1903. The measure of 1907, mentioned in somewhat more detail the regulations covering sanitary requirements of barber shops. The amendment of 1915 was relative to the powers of the board to revoke certificates. The State Board of Barber Examiners may revoke the certificate of registration granted by it to a person practicing barbering on the following

[1]Clark, L. D., The Law of the Employment of Labor, pp. 112-116.
[2]Utah, Laws 1896, C. 173.
[3]Utah, Laws 1903, C. 137.
[4]The examination fee to obtain a certificate of registration is $5.00. The annual license fee for barber shops is $1.50.
[5]Utah, Laws 1907, C. 154.
[6]Utah, Laws 1915, C. 18.
[7]Utah, Laws 1919, C. 3.
[8]Utah, Laws 1921, C. 5.

grounds: (a) conviction of crime; (b) habitual drunkenness; (c) gross incompetency; (d) the keeping of a shop or the tools, appliances or furnishings thereof in an unclean and unsanitary condition. The law of 1919 changed the age of the applicant for a certificate from sixteen to eighteen years of age, and made the compensation of each member of the board $5 per day for actual service and 10 cents for each mile actually traveled in attending to the duties of the Board. It had formerly been $4 per day for actual service. The last amendment of 1921 required the person practicing barbering in the state to not knowingly serve a person afflicted with any contagious or infectious disease but to report the case to the state board of health or local health officers.

(3) TRANSPORTATION

It is clear that the safety and welfare of both fellow servant and the public is dependent upon the efficiency of common carriers and public utilities operating within the state.

A law was passed in 1917[1] creating a Public Utilities Commission. This Commission was given jurisdiction over all public utilities within the state—state railways, express companies, street railways, telephone companies, etc.

The Commission is charged with the duty of seeing that "every public utility shall furnish, provide, and maintain such service . . . . . . equipment and facilities as shall promote, the health, comfort and convenience of its patrons, employees, and the public and as shall be in all respects adequate, efficient, just and reasonable."

(4) RESIDENT LABORERS—ALIENS

In 1894, the territorial assembly passed an act[2] appropriating money for employment of needy workmen on the capitol grounds, stipulating in the measure that as far as possible men with families and bonafide residents of the territory be given preference.

In 1909, a law[3] was passed in reference to the employment of citizens of the United States on public works. In contract for the construction of public works preference was to be given to

[1]Utah, Laws 1917, C. 47.
[2]Utah, Laws 1894, C. 10.
[3]Utah, Laws 1909, C. 80.

citizens of the United States or those declaring their intention of becoming citizens.[1]

(5) CONVICT LABOR

Restrictions in Utah, in regard to the subject of convict labor, date back to the Constitution. The State Constitution prohibits the contracting of convict labor or the use of convicts outside prison grounds except on public works under the direct control of the state.[2]

The legislature passed an act in 1909[3] restricting the employment of convicts to labor on highways, and further prohibited the use of convicts whose sentence of imprisonment was for ten or more years. Again, provision was made in the measure that the number in any construction group was not to be less than fifteen nor more than fifty. Additional good time allowance was granted to convicts so employed.

In 1911,[5] the law of 1909 was repealed and a somewhat more extended measure enacted. Not only were convicts allowed, under certain conditions, to work on or construct and improve roads, but also to be utilized in providing material for roads. In other respects, however, the provisions of the law were very similar to those stated in the earlier law of 1909.

2. THE STATE BUREAU OF STATISTICS

In Chapter II, attention was called to the enactment, passed

---

[1]Mr. Lindley Clark states that such "laws discriminating against aliens or non residents are not favored by the courts since the fourteenth amendment is held to protect with its equality clause all persons in the United States without regard to citizenship."

He also mentions the fact that the court held the law of Pennsylvania wherein employment on public works was restricted to citizens, as not valid (Philadelphia v. McLinden 205 Pa. S. 172) likewise, the New York statute giving preference to resident laborers and citizens on municipal undertakings, was held as not binding on contractors. (People v. Warren, 13 Misc. 618, 34 N. Y. Sup. 942.)

In California, Oregon and Illinois, Mr. Clark points out the courts have taken the same view. (See Clark, Lindley D., The Law of the Employment of Labor, pp. 118-119.)

[2]State Constitution of Utah, Art. 16, Sections 2 and 3.

[3]Various states of the Union have laws which restrict the labor of convicts to certain forms of industry usually to labor on public works and roadways or to the manufacture of supplies used by the state. The object is to put some restraint on competition between convict and free labor.

[4]Utah, Laws 1909, C. 96.

[5]Utah, Laws 1911, C. 76.

by the territorial assembly, creating a Bureau of Labor Statistics.

For a number of years, however, the activities of the department were somewhat curtailed by the rather meager funds provided, so that its work was confined largely to the collection of information relative to the industrial resources of the State. In 1911, the legislature enlarged the functions of the bureau and placed upon it the duty of investigating conditions of employment with the purpose in view of improving the conditions of manual laborers in general.

3. STATE INDUSTRIAL COMMISSION OF UTAH

In 1917, a further development was made in the creation of a State Industrial Commission.[1] This Commission was given all the duties, powers and privileges which had formerly been conferred and imposed by law upon the Commissioner of Immigration, Labor and Statistics.

Section 16 of Chapter 100, Laws of Utah, 1917, gives the duties and powers of the Commission as follows:

"(1) To administer and enforce all laws for the protection of life, health, safety and welfare of employees.

"(2) To ascertain and fix such reasonable standards and prescribe, modify and enforce such reasonable orders for the adoption of safety devices, safeguards and other means or methods of protection, to be as nearly uniform as possible, as may be necessary to carry out all laws and lawful orders relative to the protection of the life, health, safety and welfare of employees in employment and places of employment.

"(3) To ascertain, fix and order such reasonable standards for the construction, repair and maintenance of places of employment as shall render them safe.

"(4) To investigate, ascertain and determine such reasonable classifications of persons, employments and places of employment as shall be necessary to carry out the purposes of this Act.

"(5) To do all in its power to promote the voluntary arbitration, mediation and conciliation of disputes between employers and employees.

"(6) To establish and conduct free employment agencies, and license and supervise the work of private employment offices and to do all in its power to bring together employers seeking em-

[1] Utah, Laws 1917, C. 100.

ployees and working people seeking employment, and to make known the opportunities for employment in this State.

"(7) To collect, collate and publish all statistical and other information relating to employees, employers, employments and places of employment and such other statistics as it may deem proper.

"(8) Upon petition by any person that any employment or place of employment is not safe or is injurious to the welfare of any employee, the commission shall proceed with or without notice to make such investigation as may be necessary to determine the matter complained of. After such investigation, the commission shall enter such order relative thereto as may be necessary to render such employment or place of employment safe and not injurious to the welfare of the employees therein.

"Whenever the commission shall believe that any employment or place of employment is not safe or is injurious to the welfare of any employee, it may of its own motion summarily investigate the same, with or without notice, and issue such order as it may deem necessary to render such employment or place of employment safe.

"(9) All duties, liabilities, authority, powers and privileges conferred and imposed by law upon the commissioner of immigration, labor and statistics, state mine inspector of coal and hydro-carbon mines, and board of conciliation and arbitration are hereby imposed upon the commission.

"All laws relating to the commissioner of immigration, labor and statistics, state mine inspector of coal and hydro-carbon mines, and board of conciliation and arbitration shall apply to, relate, and refer to the Industrial Commission of Utah. The Industrial Commission of Utah shall be deemed the commissioner of immigration, labor and statistics, state mine inspector of coal and hydro-carbon mines, and board of labor, conciliation and arbitration within the meaning of existing laws.

"(10) All orders of the commission in conformity with law shall be valid and in force and prima facie reasonable and lawful until they are found otherwise in an action brought for that purpose pursuant to the provisions of this Act or until altered or revoked by the commission.

"(11) All general orders of the commission shall take effect within thirty days after their publication. Special orders shall take effect as therein directed:

"The commission shall, upon application of any employer, grant such time as may be reasonably necessary for compliance with any order.

"Any person may petition the commission for an extension of time which the commission shall grant if it finds such extension of time necessary."

The Commission is divided into three departments with a commissioner at the head of each department, and these three departments as now organized are as follows: (1) department of safety; (2) department pertaining to insurance matters; (3) department of labor, claims for compensation and labor mediation and conciliation.

The Commission has been given assistance in carrying out its work so that at the present time, there are six inspectors and an official staff of about twelve members.

4. INDUSTRIAL DISPUTES

(1) STATE BOARD OF CONCILIATION AND ARBITRATION

A word further may be said at this point relative to the Board of Conciliation and Arbitration which functioned under the jurisdiction of the Commissioner of Labor and later, assigned to the Industrial Commission.

Utah embodied in its Constitution a provision for such a board for the voluntary arbitration of industrial disputes. Sections 1 and 2, Article 16, of the State Constitution are pertinent to this subject and therefore are quoted here in full.

Section 1 provides that, "The rights of labor shall have just protection through laws calculated to promote the industrial welfare of the state".

Section 2 states that, "The Legislature shall provide by law for a Board of Labor, Conciliation and Arbitration which shall fairly represent the interests of both capital and labor. The Board shall perform duties and receive compensation as prescribed by law."

This question received considerable attention in the constitutional convention of the state before it was embodied into the Constitution. An opinion prevailed at that time that while Utah had not suffered from any serious strikes and labor troubles, the industrial life of the state was growing and therefore a general provision enabling the legislature to create such a board would undoubtedly be fruitful of good.[1]

Several neighboring states, Idaho and Wyoming, had placed similar provisions in their constitutions and their example somewhat influenced the convention in its deliberations in regard to this matter.

The legislature, in 1896,[2] carried out the provisions of the State Constitution and appointed a Board of Labor, Conciliation and Arbitration. The Governor, with the consent of the Senate appointed three members on this board—the personnel of which consisted of one employer of labor, one employee and a third member to act as chairman of the board who was neither an employer nor an employee. The members were to receive as compensation $3 a day and expenses.

The act provided only for voluntary arbitration, so the board served largely in an advisory capacity. When controversy or difference arose between employers and employees and upon application of the parties to the dispute, they made inquiry into the cause of difference hearing all persons interested and advising the respective parties what ought to be done to adjust the dispute.

Upon application for arbitration both parties to the controversy were to agree to abstain from a strike or lockout until a decision was rendered by the board which was to be made within three weeks of the time of application for arbitration. Further, said decision of the board was to be made public.

Enforcement.—No provision was made for the enforcement of the awards except the decision was binding upon the parties until either party had given the other notice in writing of his or their intention not to be bound by the same.

Investigation.—When ever it came to the notice of the board of a strike or lockout seriously threatened in the state, involving any company employing more than ten men, said board was to put itself in communication with the parties to the controversy and endeavor by mediation to effect an amicable settlement, or to have the parties submit the matter to arbitration.

Act of 1901.—The enactment, passed in 1896, was repealed

[1]Proceedings of the Constitutional Convention of Utah, 1895, Vol. II, pp. 1163-1176.
[2]Utah, Laws 1896, C. 62.

by the legislature in 1901 and a somewhat expanded law enacted,[1] but with similar provisions.

The duties of the board were given in more detail and the compensation of each member of the board was raised from $3 to $4 a day and traveling expenses incurred during the time of service in connection with any industrial dispute.

Upon the creation of the State Industrial Commission in 1917, the duties of the Board of Arbitration were assigned to this Commission.

The act creating a State Board of Conciliation and Arbitration seems quite formidable on the statute books, but the board for which it provides has exercised but little influence in the adjustment of labor disputes. In fact, it was about fifteen years after the act was passed before any cases were tried by the Board of Arbitration.

This failure to function may possibly have been due either to the lack of confidence on the part of one side or the other in a dispute to rely upon a decision of the board, or to the lack of activity on the part of the board, which received no salary except an allowance of $4 per day and traveling expenses incurred during the time of service in connection with any industrial dispute.

Since the Industrial Commission has been assigned the duties of the Board of Mediation and Arbitration, it seems to have succeeded in securing the confidence of both employer and employee, and thus has been able to do good work in a number of disputes.[2]

[1]Utah, Laws 1901, C. 68.

[2]The report of the Industrial Commission for the period July 1, 1917 to June 30, 1918, p. 14, states: "The Department of Mediation, Conciliation and Arbitration was called upon to adjudicate a total of twenty-eight labor disputes. Eight of the disputes were settled without a strike, seven disputes were settled after the men were out on strike; eight disputes were referred to the United States Department of Labor for adjudication ;in one dispute the Commission was unable to effect a satisfactory settlement; and in three disputes both parties agreed to submit to arbitration, in two of which a member of the Commission was requested by both parties, to serve on the Board of Arbitration. The Commission has sat as a Board of Arbitration in one case.

The report of the Industrial Commission for the period July 1, 1918, to June 30, 1920, p. 38, likewise shows that the Commission, during this period has had a substantial measure of success in the settlements of controversies. Of the disputes the Commission had official notice, "Twelve . . . . resulted in a strike, two of which were settled by arbitration. Four disputes were referred to the United States Department of Labor, assisted by the Commission. Three were referred to tl e War Labor Board, two were settled by arbitration without a strike."

5. INTERFERENCE WITH EMPLOYMENT

(1) INTIMIDATION

A series of laws have been enacted in the State in respect to industrial relationships between the employer and employee. A statute was enacted in 1905[1] which forbade any person, or persons, from threatening violence to any person or property for the purpose of preventing any individual, or group of persons, from engaging or remaining in any business or employment. The law made the violator guilty of a misdemeanor.

Laws of this nature embody the principles of the common law relative to conspiracy, or the unlawful infringement on the rights of others, by coercion or other improper means. While they are penal in form and effect their violation also operates to give a right of action to a party injured by the unlawful act.

Two years later, that is in 1907,[2] another measure was passed making it unlawful to interfere with the rights of any individual engaged in labor to exercise his full privileges under the Constitution of the State and under the Constitution of the United States as to where he should be employed, by whom, and at what compensation.

Again, in 1909,[3] an act was passed prohibiting any person from receiving or soliciting any sum of money on account of employment or continuing of such employment.

In a later measure passed in 1911,[4] it was made unlawful for any person to exact by threat, or coercion, any money, tribute or support, from any person; or to induce him by threats, or coercion, to join any labor organization.

In the report of the Commissioner of Labor for the years 1911-1912, protest is made in regard to padrones receiving money from foreign laborers. In advocating more adequate legislation to eradicate this practice the Commissioner writes: "The exploitation of foreign labor in this State by professional agents is an evil that should be eradicated . . . . . With some metalliferous and coal mining companies, a miner or laborer seeking employment cannot secure such until he comes with a recommendation of a padrone to whom he is obliged to pay from $25 to $50 for his job and a small sum monthly to hold the job

[1]Utah, Laws 1905, C. 16.
[2]Utah, Laws 1907, C. 76.
[3]Utah, Laws 1909, C. 52.
[4]Utah, Laws 1911, C. 74.

after it is once obtained. Many padrones secure from foreign laborers several thousand dollars each month and presumably "divy" with higher up officials under whom they are working. The peonage system is an old and mischief-making one and has been the subject of much discussion and legislation. It should be killed in this State before it secures a stronger foothold."[1]

Several of the earlier measures mentioned apply to the matter of extortion in employment, and an act passed in 1919[2] covers specifically the matter complained of in the Commissioner's report. This measure prohibits the soliciting, accepting, or receiving of gifts or money on account of employment.

(2) LABOR UNIONS

Governor Simon Bamberger in his message to the Legislature of Utah in 1917 made the following recommendation in respect to labor unions: "I . . . . . recommend . . . . the incorporation into the statutes of Utah of the provisions of the federal law securing to workingmen all rights and privileges of voluntary association for their protection and welfare, protecting their rights against unwarranted issuance of writs of injunction and guaranteeing to them the right of trial by jury in the State Courts in the case of contempt of court where the alleged offense was committed outside the presence of the court."[3]

In accord with this recommendation of the Governor of the State, Representative R. E. Curris of Salt Lake City introduced a bill which was passed by the legislature in 1917[4] which expressly recognized the right of collective bargaining. This measure, entitled, "Bettering Conditions of Labor," was one which the labor organizations throughout the state had asked the Democratic party to pass.[5]

Section I of the act provides that, "It shall not be unlawful for working men and women to organize themselves into, or carry on, labor unions[6] for the purpose of lessening the hours of labor, increasing the wages, bettering the conditions of the

[1]See Report of the State Bureau of Immigration, Labor and Statistics, 1911-1912, p. 33.
[2]Utah, Laws 1919, C. 130.
[3]House Journal, Utah 1917, p. 63.
[4]Utah, Laws 1917, C. 68.
[5]See Deseret Evening News, Feb. 16, 1917.
[6]About 25 per cent of all wage-earners in the state belong to unions. (Letter from J. J. Sullivan, Secretary and Treasurer of Utah State Federation of Labor.)

members of such organization; or carrying out their legitimate purposes as freely as they could do if acting singly."

The measure further provides that no injunctions or restraining order shall be issued from any court in the state for the purpose of preventing acts growing out of a dispute concerning terms of conditions of employment unless necessary to prevent irreparable injury to property for which there is no adequate remedy at law.

The act permits picketing during labor troubles, and the legality of strikes is also implied in this statute. It is not unlawful for any person or persons to unite or recommend or peacefully persuade others to enter into combination, to abstain from working; or from ceasing to patronize or remaining in the employment of any person or corporation or from peacefully assembling in a lawful manner or from doing an act or thing which might be done in the absence of such dispute by any party thereto.

A measure[1] was enacted two years later, in 1919, defining and prohibiting picketing in Utah.

Section 1 of the law reads: "Picketing is hereby defined to be guarding or patrolling by any citizens whomsoever, for the purpose of intercepting or persuading, or otherwise urging any person or persons whomsoever, from patronizing any duly and regularly licensed business within the State of Utah."

Section 2 reads: "Every person convicted of picketing, as defined by Section 1 of this act, shall be deemed guilty of a misdemeanor."

A large group of workers, estimated to number approximately 2500 men marched to the State Capitol on October 4, 1919, for the purpose of making protest by their presence against interference with the state law which permitted picketing by union organizations in Utah. The industrial organizations of the state, however, strongly urged the repeal of the picketing law, and they were successful in having the above mentioned law placed on the statute books.[2]

(3) BLACKLISTING

Utah also has a statute prohibiting blacklisting, the purpose being to protect employees in their natural and constitutional right to sell their labor and acquire property.

---

[1]Utah, Laws 1919, C. 19. (This act was passed in the special session of the legislature of the State of Utah which met in the fall of 1919.)
[2]See Deseret Evening News, Oct. 4, 1919.

The law[1] passed in 1896 makes it unlawful for any company, corporation or individual to publish or cause to be published, or blacklist any employee who leaves the service of such a company, voluntarily or by discharge.

Violation of this act is made a felony punishable by a fine of not less than $500, and imprisonment not less than 60 days.

(4) SYNDICALISM AND SABOTAGE

A recent law passed by the legislature in 1919[2] prohibits the advocacy, teaching, or suggestion of crime or violence, or of any unlawful act as a means to accomplish industrial or political ends. The measure further prohibits assemblages for the purpose of teaching a doctrine of criminal syndicalism or advocating sabotage.

Syndicalism is used in the law in the sense of the doctrine which advocates crime or violence, or force and the destruction of property to accomplish industrial or political ends. Sabotage is in reference to any malicious and intentional unlawful damage or destruction of real or personal property.

Penalty for violation of the act is made a felony punishable by a fine, or imprisonment, or both.

6. THE LABOR SITUATION

Just at present the labor situation in Utah is far from satisfactory, due largely to the fact that the building trades are not fully employed, and because of the reduction in the laboring force in the mining industry.

While there are no reliable statistics as to the number of men out of work, it appears that conditions of unemployment are more general now than have been experienced for some time in the state.

The prices of commodities are still high, yet there has been considerable reduction in wages. Common labor received during the war from $4 to $5 a day in certain industries. Since the war there has been a reduction arranging from 50 cents to $2, so that common labor is now generally paid about $3.75 a day.

[1]Utah, Laws 1896, C. 6.
[2]Utah, Laws 1919, C. 127.

Again it may be noted that no special provisions have been made in the state either by the public or corporations for the adequate housing of workers. Yet, the housing question is one of importance for not only large cities, but industrial communities of every size.

CHAPTER VII

SUMMARY AND CONCLUSION

In the preceding pages we have given a review of the labor laws of Utah. In this concluding chapter, our purpose will be to look back over this legislation to discover some general characteristics which seem to best show the trend of development of labor legislation in this commonwealth.

It is difficult to account for all influences at work in the enactment of the labor laws, because on some of the subjects of legislation little is published, aside from the statutes, in the way of secondary legislative material (debates, reports, and documents, etc.) It may be said generally, however, that public activity to promote the interest of laborers began with the establishment of the Bureau of Statistics.

While this bureau in the early territorial period exerted little influence in the way of promoting good conditions of work, it does mark the beginning of a movement to secure publicity concerning the conditions of labor as well as to provide the general public with useful information relative to the industrial and agricultural development in this district.

With the growth of the industry of the State, the Bureau of Statistics was enlarged and became the Bureau of Immigration, Labor, and Statistics, and likewise, its influence was increased in matters relating to the conditions of workers.

Since 1917, this branch of the State Government has been under the direction of the Industrial Commission which is charged with the duty of administering and enforcing the labor laws of the state.

In passing it may also be well to mention that the large industrial states of the Union, particularly the State of Massachusetts, have generally been regarded in advance of other states in the way of factory laws and labor legislation. In such states as Massachusetts, New York, and Pennsylvania, laborers were first brought together in large workshops and thus the need was first felt in these states for some kind of legislation to protect the welfare of wage-earners.

In the newer states of the west, or the industrially less advanced states, the tendency has been with the growth of industry to gradually adopt similar measures and in some respects, distinctly bettering conditions and going farther toward complete protection of employees.

It must also be noted that the labor legislation of Utah has also been influenced by a general movement throughout the country in the interest of the working classes. This seems to be particularly true in the case of the widows' pension law. Local conditions were not such as to render urgent an enactment of this kind, although it has been a helpful and desirable piece of legislation. On the whole, however, organized labor has been most influential in securing labor legislation. Many improvements have taken place in the condition of workers largely as a consequence of their efforts and of the economic and political power they have been able to exert. In some cases, also labor laws have come about as the direct result of abuses which the general public recognized needed correction.

The early labor laws of Utah, as our study shows, were few in number because the people for the most part were engaged in agricultural pursuits. Only as the industrial life of the state developed was attention given to the enactment of measures in the interest of labor.

In the territorial period, there seems to have been little organized effort made by any party or organization to secure such legislation. Aside from a few general measures, passed in the seventies and eighties, the early labor laws were a result of specific requirements of the State Constitution. Our account clearly shows, however, that the major portion of labor enactments have been secured in the last ten or fifteen years, particularly during the last decade.

It is also evident from our study that the labor legislation of Utah aims to promote: (1) wholesome conditions of labor; (2) security of wage-payment and the regulation of the payment of wages; (3) right of collective bargaining on the part of wage-earners to safe-guard and promote their interests; (4) relief for industrial accident on the basis of social solidarity, as seen in the workmen's compensation act.

The first object of labor legislation as mentioned above is seen in the laws establishing shorter work days and in health and safety measures. The eight-hour day in public and certain private industry (mining and smelting) is one of the accomplishments. Yet, notwithstanding the attention given to the eight-hour movement as seen in legislative enactments, possibly as much has been accomplished by collective bargaining as by legislation. At the present time, the eight-hour day is observed by nearly all employing establishments for men as well as for women.

The state likewise has concerned itself with the conserving of the lives of workers. Measures have been passed regulating mining operations and attention has been directed to the safe-guarding of machinery in factories and work shops. Inspection is being increased and the State Industrial Commission is from time to time issuing pamphlets with rules and regulations distinctly helpful in safe-guarding workers.

To guard the life and limb of laborers is of far-reaching importance and proper attention is just beginning to be given it. Recent studies made in a number of states emphasize health and safety elements in all questions of employment. The problem is large and the best efforts of the public must be put forth toward the conservation of human life.

The chief measures for the payment of wages relate to mechanics liens, the minimum wage act and protection to the wage-workers against methods of paying or computing their wages which may operate to their disadvantage.

The minimum wage act is the latest step in wage-payment legislation, but so far it is confined to women and girl apprentices, legally employed in industry. It is legislative relief against exploitation, but the standard set as a minimum wage is wholly inadequate, and so low as almost to defeat the purpose of the law.

In regard to the third object the people concede to the wage-workers the right to organize as a means of safe-guarding and promoting their interests. The attitude maintained is that labor is not a chattel, but possesses rights which should not be ignored.

On the whole, the labor movement in Utah seems to have been free from any conspicuously arbitrary policy. While the activities of organized labor have made possible various measures which otherwise probably would not have been enacted, it would seem, from reports, that they have manifested fair mindedness in their efforts to establish justice for the workingmen of the state.[1]

[1]A recent convention of the Utah State Federation was held at Provo. The mayor of this city in welcoming the delegates paid tribute to the integrity and fairmindedness of organized labor in its efforts to improve the condition of labor within the state. (Proceedings of the Sixteenth Convention of the Utah State Federation of Labor, 1920, p. 3.)

The fourth division or purpose of labor legislation, as outlined in the preceding pages, is largely confined to the question of liability for industrial accident. Here we see, as indicated by the workmen's compensataion act, a legislative policy which introduces the principle of social solidarity. The health and welfare of the wage-earner is made a matter of public interest. An industrial accident is treated as a social phenomenon requiring remedial treatment and relief through a system of insurance.

This new phase of the legislative policy of the state is a great step in industrial betterment. It tends to maintain peace in industrial pursuits by adjusting, without court procedure and legal battles, financial losses inflicted upon workmen by industrial accidents and furthermore it serves as a stimulus to the whole safety movement.

At this point in our summary, it may be well to turn our attention to the methods of administration and enforcement of labor measures. This may justly be considered one of the most important problems of labor legislation, because the results attained depend largely upon the way the laws are enforced.

It is proverbial that American legislatures pass laws freely, so a large body of laws may only be a partial proof that good working conditions are assured. Various writers on this subject have pointed out that more important than the hasty enactment of laws is the adoption of methods of administration which will make the laws effective in actual practice.[1]

Utah's statutes reflect certain consideration of the difficulties of administration encountered in the actual working of the labor laws. They reveal a number of provisions intended to put the laws into operation. In the case of the early laws it was left to local officials to attend to the prosecutions on complaint; secondly, provision was made for the appointment of special state agents to enforce the laws; and, thirdly, an industrial commission was established to enforce all the labor laws.

The existence of provisions imposing penalties does not of itself assure obedience. Prohibition even with a threat of punishment is often a weak barrier to prevent wilful or ignorant violation of law.

---

[1]Commons and Andrews point out in their book, Principles of Labor Legislation, p. 449, that, "it is easy for politicians, or reformers, or trade union officials to boast of the laws which they have secured for labor, and it is just as easy to overlook the details, or appropriations, or competent officials, that are needed to make them enforceable."

Again, the results are usually small where local officials, with no special responsibility to see that the laws are obeyed, are depended upon to secure their observance. Injured employees are often reticent in making complaint for fear of being discharged; and again, local officials have other duties regarded as more urgent.

In time the futility of this kind of administration was discovered, and the next step was the appointment (usually by the governor) of special officials or inspectors[1] whose duty it was to ascertain that the laws were observed.

This method tended to put the enforcement of the laws upon a new basis, for these state agents make inspection on their own initiative and do not act upon complaints only. For various reasons,[2] however, the enforcement of labor laws by special inspectors, working in connection with different state departments, has come to be recognized as not satisfactory, so the most recent step in administration has been to create a state industrial commission;[3] a central agency enforcing all labor laws.

The duties of this commission have been already pointed out in some detail in an earlier chapter, especially in connection with the workmen's compensation act, so probably further comment here is not necessary. Suffice it to say that the commission gives promise of consistent work. Its usefulness, however, will depend in great measure upon its working staff. If there are too many duties for the men employed it will hardly be able to do more than keep in touch with the various lines of industrial activity which it ought to oversee and control.[4]

In this summary, let it also be said that the employers of the state are generally in sympathy with the labor laws and have little fault to find with them. It is only the small minority which show any tendency to violate or evade the laws.

[1]For a number of years the inspection in Utah, in so far as it relates to labor, was confined largely to mining and smelting operations, of late years, however, it has also included factory inspection.

[2]The number of inspectors is often inadequate for the work required; and again, they are often not trained for their work.

[3]This plan is in line with the trend of modern labor legislation, for a number of the states now have their labor laws enforced by so-called industrial commissions.

[4]The trade unions of the state and certain philanthropic organizations, generally the same ones which have been active in securing the enactment of the laws, assist to some extent in the administration of the labor laws.

On the whole, the labor laws have been of great benefit to the laboring classes and have improved their condition and the conditions under which they work very materially. The good results especially of woman and child labor laws, the hours legislation, bi-monthly payments and the workingmen's compensation act stand out most clearly.

While advancement has been made in establishing laws looking toward the improvement of working conditions, this should not mean complacent optimism, for progress in industry must come from continuous growth and change.

While at present there is no imperative call for unfilled gaps in a general scheme of protective labor legislation in the state the matter of the minimum wage law should receive further attention, and be amended.[1] Women who are entirely dependent upon their wages for support find little protection in the present law. If it is to serve its purpose, it ought to be revised along the lines of changing the flat-rate system to a board or commission type. This would allow for the adjustment of rates as conditions in the various industries seem to warrant. Most students of the problem of wage-adjustment concede that this is a better plan than to rely upon a flat-rate method.

It seems probable, also, that the trend in labor legislation will be in the direction of an expansion of the principle of social insurance. So far in Utah, and many other states, it has not gone much beyond accident insurance and widows' pensions. In time it may include occupational diseases, sickness insurance, and unemployment benefits. This, however, does not mean paternal legislation, but legislation most in accord with the need of modern industry.

European countries have for a number of years experimented with this plan of social insurance and have found it valuable, and helpful to workers in general.

Further development may also be along the line of delegating power to administrative commissions; that is to say, the substituting of administrative rules for legislative details. An

[1]J. J. Sullivan, Secretary and Treasurer of the Utah State Federation of Labor advocates a state law providing a minimum wage that will sustain the worker and his family in health and reasonable comfort. At the present time the minimum wage law applies only to the female wage-earners. He also advocates a law establishing a universal eight hour day for all workers and a law establishing one day of rest in seven for all workers as well as an expansion of the principle of social insurance for all workers. (Letters from J. J. Sullivan, Secretary and Treasurer of the Utah State Federation of Labor.)

advantage often mentioned in connection with this plan is that rule-making is more scientific than statute-making because commissioners are more likely to be better trained and informed than legislative bodies.

Possibly as yet there has been too little experience with rule-making to settle what ought to be determined by statute and what matters to leave to regulations. Progress in this direction may well be watched with interest.

We are not to infer that legislation is designed to be a cure-all-plan for industrial relations. Other factors are of importance in connection with this question, but to comment on these factors brings us to the fringe of the problems of our industrial order in general.

There is no intention here to elaborate on the country's policy in regard to industrial problems. Suffice it to say in this connection that it would seem as we reach out for some invention or new mechanism to make reason triumphant in international relations that we shall witness a creation of institutions to establish industrial good-will.

BIBLIOGRAPHY

PRIMARY SOURCES:

Constitution of Utah, ratified, 1896.

House Journals, Utah, 1915 and 1917.

Proceedings of the Constitutional Convention, Vol. 2, pp. 1061-1068 and pp. 1163-1176.

Reports of the State Bureau of Immigration, Labor, and Statistics,

YEARS:

1911-1912
1913-1914
1915-1916

Reports of the Industrial Commission of Utah

YEARS:

1917-1918
1919-1920

Statutes of Utah:

Session Laws for the Territorial Period, 1950-1896.
Session Laws for the Period of Statehood, 1896-1921.

Thirteenth Census of the United States, 1910, (Principally the Supplement on Utah.)

Fourteenth Census of the United States, 1920, (Principally advanced bulletins on Agriculture, Manufacturing and Population.)

SECONDARY SOURCES:

American Association for Labor Legislation, (American Labor Legislation Review.) Review of Labor Legislation of 1919, December, 1919.

Bancroft, H. H., History of Utah, 1540-1886, San Francisco, The History Company, 1889. (Principally Chapters 27 and 28, dealing with the industrial resources of Utah—Agriculture, manufacturing, mining, commerce, and communication.)

Commons, John R., and Andrews, John B., Principles of Labor Legislation, New York, Harper & Bros., Rev. ed. 1920.

Clark, Lindley D., The Law of the Employment of Labor, New York, Macmillan, 1911.

Paxson, F. L., The Last American Frontier, New York, Macmillan, 1910.

Proceedings of the Fifteenth Convention of the Utah State Federation of Labor, 1919.

Proceedings of the Sixteenth Convention of the Utah State Federation of Labor, 1920.

Tullidge, Edward W., Life of Brigham Young; or Utah and Her Founders, New York, 1876. (Principally Chapter 13, Pictures of Mormon Society in the Founding of Utah.)

United States Bureau of Labor Statistics, Bulletin No. 240, Comparison of Workmen's Compensation Laws of the United States to December 31, 1917.

United States, Final Report of the Commission on Industrial Relations. (Reprinted from Senate Doc. No. 415, 64th Congress, Washington, Govt. Printing Office, 1916.

Whitney, Orson F., Popular History of Utah, Salt Lake City, Utah, The Deseret News, 1916.

Young, Levi E., The Story of Utah, Instructor Literature Series, No. 542, Chicago, Hall & McCreary, 1913.

Table of Cases Cited:

The following cases have been cited in this study:

D. & R. G. R. Co., v. Grand County, 51 U. 294, (1914.)

Holden v. Hardy, 169 U. S. 366, 18 Sup. Ct., 564, (1898.)

Industrial Commission of Utah v. Daly Mining Co., 51 U. 602, (1918).

Nashville, C. & St. L. Ry. v. Alabama, 128 U. S. 96, 9 Sup. Ct. 28

Phil. v. McLinden, 205 Pa. S. 172, 54 Atl. 719.

People v. Warren, 13 Misc. 618, 34 N. Y. Supt. 942.

State v. Briggs, 45 Oregon 366, 77 Pac. 750.

Saville v. Corless 46 U. 495, (1915.)

Stettler v. O'Hara, 60 Ore. 519, (1914.)

Stettler v. O'Hara, 243 U. S. 629, 37 Sup. Ct. 475, (1917.)

Utah v. Holden, 14 U. 71.

Utah v. Holden, 14 U. 96.

Utah Copper Co. v. Industrial Commission, 193 Pac. 24.

Utah Fuel Co. v. Industrial Commission, 194 Pac. 122.

VITA

The writer of this dissertation was born in 1882, at Ephraim, Utah. He received from the University of Utah, the degree of A. B., in 1912, and that of A. M., in 1915. He was a graduate student at the University of California during the summer of 1913, and at the University of Chicago during the summer quarter of 1917.

During the school year of 1915-16, he was principal of the Moroni High School, at Moroni, Utah, and the following year he was appointed principal of the Wasatch County High School at Heber City, Utah. In 1917, he received the appointment as principal of the Weber Normal College at Ogden, Utah. In 1919 he resigned this position to take up his study at Columbia University where he was in residence two years, until the fall of 1921.

At Columbia University, he studied principally under Professors Lindsay, Giddings, Chaddock, Seager, Tenney, and Ogburn, and he attended the seminars of Professor Lindsay and Giddings.

In 1921, he accepted the position as head of the social science department of the Brigham Young College at Logan, Utah, a position that he now holds.